PRAYERS IN HONOR OF
SAINT THOMAS AQUINAS

PRAYERS
in Honor of
Saint Thomas Aquinas

Compiled by
THOMAS O'SULLIVAN

Os Justi
Press

Copyright © 2025 Thomas O'Sullivan
All rights reserved.

No part of this book may be reproduced, stored in a retrieval system, or transmitted in any form, or by any means, electronic, mechanical, photocopying, or otherwise, without the prior written permission of the publisher, except by a reviewer, who may quote brief passages in a review.

Os Justi Press
P.O. Box 21814
Lincoln, NE 68542
www.osjustipress.com

Send inquiries to
info@osjustipress.com

ISBN 978-1-965303-26-9 (paperback)
ISBN 978-1-965303-36-8 (hardcover)

Nihil obstat: Fr. Evan Winter, Censor librorum
Imprimatur: ✠ Most Rev. James D. Conley
Bishop of Lincoln
July 4, 2025

Layout and cover by Michael Schrauzer
Cover illustration based on a print by Michel Natalis, after a painting by Abraham van Diepenbeeck, ca. 1650.
Original image: https://id.rijksmuseum.nl/200237230

Sancto Thomæ Aquinati
Doctori Angelico
in gratiarum actionem

25. *E. van Panderen.*

Ad Concilium Lugduni indictum se conferens, in itinere morbo correptus ad cœnobium Fossæ-nouæ Cistertiensis Ord. diuertit, vbi cùm vltimum instare sibi diem prospiceret, fratribus illius loci Cantica Canticorum exposuit. Verùm cum ad ea verba, Veni dilecte mi, &c. peruenisset, oculis in cælum sublatis, spiritum Deo reddidit. Visus est eodem momento Religioso cuidam S. Petrus Apost. qui Thomam è schola ad cælum trahere videbatur. Quin et Albertus Magnus Coloniæ existens, lacrymans adstantibus dixit, F. Thomas de Aquino Ecclesiæ lumen hodie exspirauit.

CONTENTS

Preface xi

The Little Office of Saint Thomas Aquinas. 2
Antiphons and Responsories from the Office of
    Saint Thomas Aquinas. 56
Prayer of the Angelic Warfare Confraternity 66
Prayers to Saint Thomas,
    Patron of Catholic Schools 68
Prayer Before Studying Saint Thomas 70
Litany in Honor of Saint Thomas Aquinas,
    Doctor of the Church and Patron of Chastity . . 72
The Six Sundays in Honor
    of Saint Thomas Aquinas 85

Sources 95

Cùm eum aliquando nutrix in balneo abluere vellet, infans chartulam
è terris sublatam (in qua Salutatio Angelica descripta erat) quanta
vi potuit pugno clauso retinuit; quam cum violenter nutrix abstu=
lisset, fletu et clamore eam infans repetijt, quam acceptam ori ingerens
deglutijt: vt iam à teneris annis coluisse Deiparam visus sit.

PREFACE

JULY 18, 2023, SAW THE SEVEN HUNDREDTH anniversary of the canonization of Saint Thomas Aquinas by Pope John XXII. March 7, 2024, was the seven hundred and fiftieth anniversary of the Angelic Doctor's passing to heaven. Finally, 2025 sees the (probable) eight hundredth anniversary of his birth. Being blessed to have Saint Thomas as my patron and owing my conversion to Catholicism to the study of his teaching, I was hoping to find some way to honor him during these anniversary years. Providentially, a thought came to me during meditation when beginning the devotion of the six Sundays in preparation for his feast; namely, that I should try to find a way to reprint the Little Office of Saint Thomas, as it has not been easy to find it. I contacted Dr. Peter Kwasniewski for advice, and the result of that correspondence is this book.

This Little Office was indulgenced by Leo XIII, the pope who did so much to restore Thomism, though the indulgences no longer apply. It is very short (usually using only parts of psalms rather than whole ones) and thus could make an excellent devotion for those interested in structuring their day around the Church's hours of prayer but whose circumstances do not allow them to take up the canonical Office or the Little Office of the Blessed Virgin Mary. Yet there is no reason why those, too, who already pray the Office could not, for devotional reasons — e.g., in the lead-up to the Angelic Doctor's feast — adopt this devotion.[1] For the sake of those used to reciting an Office according to the Roman rite, it should be noted that this Little Office is based on the Dominican rite, which differs in some respects from the Roman: the antiphons are recited only *after* the psalms and canticles; the lessons are always introduced with *Jube domne* and end with *miserere nostri*, not *nobis* (the verb *misereor* taking either the dative or the genitive); there is a responsory as well as the *Te Deum* after the final lesson at Matins; a versicle and response come between Matins and Lauds; the sign of the Cross is not made when beginning the *Benedictus*, *Magnificat*, and *Nunc Dimittis*; the collect includes the words *atque Doctóris*.

The sources for the texts are listed at the end of the volume. Some changes have been made for the sake of uniformity of spelling and for accuracy. Many of the texts of the Little Office are taken from the Dominican office for the feasts of Saint Thomas (in addition to his principal feast on the *dies natalis* of March 7, the Dominicans for many years kept the feast of the translation of his relics to Toulouse on January 28; for several years in the twentieth century, this was replaced by the feast of his patronage over Catholic schools on November 13); the remaining antiphons and responsories from those

---

[1] This Little Office is a private devotion that may be added to, but cannot replace or substitute for, any official breviary or liturgy of the hours.

feasts are printed in the section following the Little Office. They can be used as short prayers in honor of Saint Thomas or to compose a novena.

The translation of the Little Office is mostly by Newman's great friend Fr. Ambrose St. John, but I have changed the Scriptural texts to match the Douay-Rheims (since Fr. St. John was a bit inconsistent), fixed a couple of inaccuracies, and made other language more consistent (mostly the archaic third-person singular endings). The extra antiphons/responsories are mostly my own translations, apart from one by Dr. Michael Foley. The translation of the Angelic Warfare Confraternity Prayer and the Six Sundays prayers are all from the old English translation of Fr. Pflugbeil's *St. Thomas Manual*. The prayer "Angelic Doctor" to Saint Thomas as patron of Catholic Schools is from the 1957 *Raccolta*. Spelling and capitalization has sometimes been altered for consistency. The short prayer "O Saint Thomas, patron of schools" is my own translation from the Latin in the 1903 *Raccolta*. The Litany in English is also my translation, apart from the first prayer at the end, which is just that of Fr. St. John taken from the Office, but with the words "and Doctor" removed to match the Latin text (the Roman rite Collect of Saint Thomas curiously doesn't use the title "doctor" but the Dominican rite does, hence the discrepancy). Petitions in the Litany that are quotations or paraphrases of Scripture use the Douay-Rheims, and petitions that are common to all litanies are taken from the 1957 *Raccolta*.

Thanks are due to Father Dominic Jacob of the Oxford Oratory, the staff of the Bodleian Library at the University of Oxford, the libraries of the University of Toronto, Google Books, and Internet Archive for making available various texts used in this book. I would also like to thank Dr. Peter Kwasniewski for providing the text of the Prayer before Studying Saint Thomas and for all his help in producing this work.

I hope this modest pamphlet will help to spread devotion to Saint Thomas Aquinas, the Angelic Doctor, whose holiness and learning are much needed for the strengthening of the inner man and for defense against the sins and errors of the modern age. For we should never forget that we are dealing with a holy man, a disciple of Christ, a miracle-worker, an intercessor before the throne of God, a powerful member of the Mystical Body in its heavenly glory. The prayers contained in this volume will help us relate to Saint Thomas first and foremost as the Lord's beloved friend, which can only enhance our use of the legacy he has left behind in this vale of tears.

Eo tempore quo Manichæorum dogmata oppugnabat, S. Ludouicus Rex Galliæ eum ad comuniam inuitauit. Prioris quidem iussu eò se contulit, at inter epulas adeò studijs intentus erat, vt manu mensam percutiens diceret, **Definitum est contra Manichæos**, vocansque ex nomine socium, *Surge*, ait, *et scribe*. Dicente porro Priore non se domi sed in mensa regia versari, veniam à Rege petijt.

Cùm graui disceptatione de Ven. Sacramento Eucharistiæ orta, Thomas sententiam
suam scripto consignasset, eamque in altari coram Crucifixo posuisset, orans vt eam
Christus signo aliquo confirmaret; ecce tibi subitò Thomam à terra sublimem, Cruci-
fixumque ad eum clara voce dicentem: Benè scripsisti de me, Thoma,
quam ergo mercedem accipies? Cui ille, Non aliam nisi te, Domine.

PRAYERS
in Honor of
Saint
Thomas Aquinas

OFFICIUM PARVUM SANCTI THOMÆ AQUINATIS

AD MATUTINUM.

℣. Dómine, lábia mea apéries.
℟. Et os meum annuntiábit laudem tuam.
℣. Deus in adjutórium meum inténde.
℟. Dómine ad adjuvándum me festína.
Glória Patri, et Fílio, et Spirítui Sancto.
Sicut erat in princípio, et nunc, et semper, et in sǽcula sæculórum. Amen.

.....
INVITATORIUM.

Laudémus Deum nostrum, * in commemoratióne Sancti Thomæ.

PS. XCIV. Veníte, exsultémus Dómino, jubilémus Deo, salutári nostro: præoccupémus fáciem ejus in confessióne, et in psalmis jubilémus ei.

Laudémus Deum nostrum, in commemoratióne Sancti Thomæ.

Glória Patri, et Fílio, et Spirítui Sancto.—In commemoratióne Sancti Thomæ.

.....
HYMNUS.

Exsúltet mentis júbilo
Laudans turba fidélium,

THE LITTLE OFFICE OF SAINT THOMAS AQUINAS

AT MATINS.

℣. O Lord, thou wilt open my lips.
℟. And my mouth shall declare thy praise.
℣. O God, come to my assistance.
℟. O Lord, make haste to help me.

Glory be to the Father, and to the Son, and to the Holy Ghost.

As it was in the beginning, is now, and ever shall be, world without end. Amen.

.....

INVITATORY.

Let us praise God * in the commemoration of Saint Thomas.

PS. XCIV. O come, let us be glad in the Lord, let us joyfully sing to the God of our salvation; let us come before his presence with thanksgiving, and make a joyful noise to him in psalms.

Let us praise God in the commemoration of Saint Thomas.

Glory be to the Father, and to the Son, and to the Holy Ghost.—In the commemoration of Saint Thomas.

.....

HYMN.

Now let the faithful crowd
Exulting pour its lay;

Errórum pulso núbilo
Per novi solis rádium.

Thomas in mundi véspere
Fudit thesáuros grátiæ,
Donis plenus ex æthere
Morum et sapiéntiæ.

Laus Patri sit ac Génito,
Simúlque sancto Flámini,
Qui sancti Thomæ mérito
Nos cæli jungat ágmini.
Amen.

.....

PSALMUS I.

Beátus vir, qui non ábiit in consílio impiórum, et in via peccatórum non stetit, * et in cáthedra pestiléntiæ non sedit:

Sed in lege Dómini volúntas ejus, * et in lege ejus meditábitur die ac nocte.

Et erit tamquam lignum, quod plantátum est secus decúrsus aquárum, * quod fructum suum dabit in témpore suo:

Et fólium ejus non défluet: * et ómnia quæcúmque fáciet, prosperabúntur.

Glória Patri, et Fílio, * et Spirítui Sancto.

Sicut erat in princípio, et nunc, et semper, * et in sǽcula sæculórum. Amen.

Ant. Florem pudicítiæ servans illibátum, áttigit exímiæ vitæ cælibátum.

Dispersing error's cloud,
Behold a new sun's ray.

Thomas when night was nigh
Shone out, and did not faint,
Illumined from on high,
Philosopher and Saint.

Praise to the Father be,
Praise to the Son and Spirit,
For Thomas' sake, may we
Heaven's company inherit.
Amen.

.....

PSALM I.

Blessed is the man who hath not walked in the counsel of the ungodly, nor stood in the way of sinners, * nor sat in the chair of pestilence:

But his will is in the law of the Lord, * and on his law he shall meditate day and night.

And he shall be like a tree which is planted near the running waters, * which shall bring forth its fruit, in due season.

And his leaf shall not fall off: * and all whatsoever he shall do shall prosper.

Glory be to the Father, and to the Son, * and to the Holy Ghost.

As it was in the beginning, is now, and ever shall be, * world without end. Amen.

Ant. Preserving spotless the flower of chastity, he attained the purity of a favored life.

℣. Amávit eum Dóminus et ornávit eum.
℟. Stolam glóriæ índuit eum.

Pater noster, qui es in cælis, sanctificétur nomen tuum. Advéniat regnum tuum. Fiat volúntas tua, sicut in cælo et in terra. Panem nostrum quotidiánum da nobis hódie. Et dimítte nobis débita nostra, sicut et nos dimíttimus debitóribus nostris.
℣. Et ne nos indúcas in tentatiónem.
℟. Sed líbera nos a malo.

℣. Jube domne benedícere.
Oret piis précibus pro nobis Doctor Angélicus.
℟. Amen.

.....
LECTIO I.

Beátus Doctor Thomas fuit typus et exémplar omnis virtútis. Omnia córporis membra erant in eo manifésta virtútum exémpla: in óculis ejus apparébat simplícitas, in fácie benígnitas, in áuribus humílitas, in incéssu grávitas, in gestu honéstas, in viscéribus píetas, in intelléctu cláritas, in afféctu bónitas, in mente sánctitas, in corde cáritas. Ad istud ergo perfectíssimum omnis virtútis exémplar mentes nostras frequénter convertámus: quod non solum doctrínæ lucem, sed étiam amórem sanctitátis in nos transfúndat. Tu autem Dómine miserére nostri. ℟. Deo grátias.

℣. The Lord loved him and adorned him.
℟. He clothed him with a robe of glory.

Our Father who art in heaven, hallowed be thy name. Thy kingdom come. Thy will be done on earth as it is in heaven. Give us this day our daily bread. And forgive us our trespasses, as we forgive those who trespass against us.
℣. And lead us not into temptation.
℟. But deliver us from evil.

℣. Pray, Father, give the blessing.
Blessing. May the Angelic Doctor offer for us his pious prayers.
℟. Amen.

.....
FIRST LESSON.

The blessed Doctor Thomas was the type and model of all virtues. All the members of his body were manifest examples of holiness. In his eyes appeared simplicity, in his face benignity, his hearing was ever humbly attentive. Gravity was in his movements, modesty in his demeanor, tender piety in his bosom, brightness in his understanding, goodness in his affections, holiness in his mind, charity in his heart. Therefore let us frequently turn our minds to this most perfect model of all virtues, so that not only the light of his doctrine but also his love of sanctity may be infused into our souls. But thou, O Lord, have mercy on us. ℟. Thanks be to God.

℟. De excélsis Fons sapiéntiæ sancto Thomæ infúdit cópiam, tamquam flumen claræ sciéntiæ: qui suscéptam refúdit grátiam, dum fluéntis summæ perítiæ * Rigat totam sanctam Ecclésiam. ℣. Stylus brevis, grata facúndia: celsa, clara, firma senténtia.—Rigat totam sanctam Ecclésiam.[1]

℣. Jube domne benedícere.
In omni perículo et angústia sit nobis pius Thomas custódia.
℟. Amen.

LECTIO II.

Perfécto vacans stúdio, intendébat Deo. Præmittébat divína ut roborarétur in schola: cum, síngulis diébus, ántequam lectúrus ascénderet cáthedram, vel distrahéretur ad ália, missam unam celebráret, áliam audíret; vel duas íntegras missas, si non celebráret, audíret: in quibus, et álias in oratióne, cum in illa foret assíduus, lacrimárum effusióne mentis suæ dulcédinem devotionémque Deo, cui nihil est abscóndicum, revelábat. Ita scholásticas, et non semel áridas, concertatiónes temperábat contemplatiónis dulcédine; ita nectébat stúdium et oratiónem, quæ falso credunt nonnúlli máxime dissidére, et mínime valére conjúngi. Tu autem Dómine miserére nostri. ℟. Deo grátias.

---

[1] This responsory seems to be based on the lecture, or *principium*, that Saint Thomas gave when made a Master at the University of Paris. Saint Thomas was instructed in a vision to use the text "Rigans montes de superioribus suis: de fructu operum tuorum satiabitur terra" (Thou

℟. Descending from heaven, the fountain of wisdom infused abundantly in Saint Thomas the waters of lucid wisdom. The grace which he received, he in turn caused to flow, as a most pure river. * He watereth every part of the holy Church. ℣. Concise in style, graceful in expression, lofty, brilliant, and solid in doctrine.—He watereth every part of the holy Church.[1]

℣. Pray, Father, give the blessing.

Blessing. In all dangers and distresses may the pious Saint Thomas be our keeper.

℟. Amen.

.....

SECOND LESSON.

In his greatest application to study he remained united to God. He applied beforehand to prayer that he might receive strength in the schools. Each day, before teaching or other employment, he celebrated Mass, and assisted at a second; if prevented from celebrating, he heard two Masses. During this holy exercise, as also in other times of prayer, which he assiduously practiced, the tears which flowed from his eyes revealed the sweetness and devotion to God, from whom nothing is hid, which filled his soul. Thus he tempered the dryness of scholastic labors with the sweetness of contemplation; thus he united study and prayer, which are wrongly considered by some to differ

---

waterest the hills from thy upper rooms: the earth shall be filled with the fruit of thy works; Ps. 103:13). His lecture uses this text as an analogy for God pouring forth the gifts of wisdom on the learned, through whom it then passes to the other members of the Church.

℟. O ánima sanctíssima, qua contemplánte dúlciter, corpus linquébat ínfima, * Stans sursum mirabíliter.
℣. Nullo prorsus fultus subsídio, levabátur in raptus gáudio. — Stans sursum mirabíliter.

℣. Jube domne benedícere.
Ad societátem cívium supernórum perdúcat nos Doctor Angélicus.
℟. Amen.

.....
LECTIO III.

Nullus enarráre suffíceret quot sanctíssimus Thomas theologórum præcóniis celebrétur: quantúmque ejus illibátæ doctrínæ a Summis Pontifícibus fúerit acclamátum. Leo autem Décimus tértius, libentíssime excípiens postulatiónes et vota ómnium pene sacrórum Antístitum orbis cathólici, ad tot præcípue philosophicórum systématum a veritáte aberrántium luem propulsándam, ad increménta scientiárum, et commúnem humáni géneris utilitátem, eum, ex sacrórum Rítuum Congregatiónis consúlto, per apostólicas lítteras cæléstem patrónum scholárum ómnium catholicárum declarávit et instítuit. Tu autem Dómine miserére nostri.
℟. Deo grátias.

℟. Sertum gestans cum torque dúplici, cappa gemmis ornáta cérnitur: ex moníli fulgóris cǽlici lux

widely from each other, and to be incompatible. But thou, O Lord, have mercy on us. ℟. Thanks be to God.

℟. O most holy soul, in the sweetness of whose contemplation the body was raised from the earth, * Resting miraculously suspended. ℣. Without any support, he was raised from the earth in a rapture of joy.—Resting miraculously suspended.

℣. Pray, Father, give the blessing.
Blessing. May the Angelic Doctor conduct us into the society of the Blessed in heaven.
℟. Amen.

.....
THIRD LESSON.

It would be impossible to relate all the magnificent eulogiums which Saint Thomas hath received from theologians, or the solemn approbations of the purity of his doctrine, pronounced by Supreme Pontiffs. Leo XIII, therefore, receiving with joy the supplications and almost unanimous desires of the episcopate; and desiring to destroy the evil of so many false philosophies, to procure the increase of science and the general good of society; after consulting the Sacred Congregation of Rites, hath, by Apostolic Letters, declared and instituted the Angelic Doctor patron of all Catholic schools. But thou, O Lord, have mercy on us. ℟. Thanks be to God.

℟. He was seen by a Friar in a vision, crowned with a diadem, wearing a magnificent chain, and a cloak covered

emíssa mundo diffúnditur: * Augustínus Fratri sic lóquitur: ℣. Thomas mihi par est in glória, virgináli præstans mundítia.—Augustínus Fratri sic lóquitur.—Gloria Patri, et Fílio, et Spirítui Sancto.—Augustínus Fratri sic lóquitur.[2]

.....
CANTICUM SS. AMBROSII ET AUGUSTINI.

Te Deum laudámus: * te Dóminum confitémur.
Te ætérnum Patrem * omnis terra venerátur.
Tibi omnes Angeli, * tibi cæli et univérsæ Potestátes.
Tibi Chérubim et Séraphim * incessábili voce proclámant:
Sanctus, Sanctus, Sanctus * Dóminus Deus Sábaoth.

℣. Ora pro nobis beáte Thoma.
℟. Ut digni efficiámur promissiónibus Christi.

---

[2] "Augustine" is Saint Augustine of Hippo. The two greatest doctors appeared together to a Brother Albert of Brescia, who had prayed

with jewels; from the chain proceeded a radiant light which was diffused over the world. * Augustine spoke thus to the Friar: ℣. Thomas is my equal in glory; he surpasseth me by virginal purity. – Augustine spoke thus to the Friar. – Glory be to the Father, and to the Son, and to the Holy Ghost. – Augustine spoke thus to the Friar.[2]

.....

CANTICLE OF SAINT AMBROSE & SAINT AUGUSTINE.

We praise thee, O God, * we acknowledge thee to be our Lord.

Thee the Father everlasting, * all the earth doth worship.

To thee all the angels; * to thee the heavens and all the powers:

To thee the Cherubim and Seraphim * continually do cry.

Holy, Holy, Holy, * Lord God of Sabaoth.

℣. Pray for us, O blessed Thomas.

℟. That we may be made worthy of the promises of Christ.

---

to be shown "the glory of Brother Thomas" (Pflugbeil, *St. Thomas Manual*, 28).

AD LAUDES.

℣. Deus in adjutórium meum inténde.
℞. Dómine ad adjuvándum me festína.
Glória Patri, et Fílio, et Spirítui Sancto.
Sicut erat in princípio, et nunc, et semper, et in sǽcula sæculórum. Amen.

PSALMUS CXVI.

Laudáte Dóminum, omnes gentes: * laudáte eum, omnes pópuli:
Quóniam confirmáta est super nos misericórdia ejus: * et véritas Dómini manet in ætérnum.
Glória Patri, et Fílio, * et Spirítui Sancto.
Sicut erat in princípio, et nunc, et semper, * et in sǽcula sæculórum. Amen.

Ant. Collaudétur Christus Rex glóriæ, qui per Thomam lumen Ecclésiæ mundum replet doctrína grátiæ.

CAPITULUM. ECCLI. XLV.

Elégit eum Dóminus ex omni carne, et dedit illi coram præcépta, et legem vitæ et disciplínæ, docére Jacob testaméntum suum, et judícia sua Israël. ℞. Deo grátias.

AT LAUDS.

℣. O God, come to my assistance.

℟. O Lord, make haste to help me.

Glory be to the Father, and to the Son, and to the Holy Ghost.

As it was in the beginning, is now, and ever shall be, world without end. Amen.

.....
PSALM CXVI.

O praise the Lord, all ye nations: * praise him, all ye people.

For his mercy is confirmed upon us: * and the truth of the Lord remaineth for ever.

Glory be to the Father, and to the Son, * and to the Holy Ghost.

As it was in the beginning, is now, and ever shall be, * world without end. Amen.

Ant. May Christ the King of Glory be praised, who by Thomas, the light of the Church, doth fill the world with the doctrine of grace.

.....
CHAPTER. ECCLUS. XLV.

The Lord chose him out of all flesh, and he gave him commandments before his face, and a law of life and instruction, that he might teach Jacob his covenant, and Israel his judgments. ℟. Thanks be to God.

.....
HYMNUS.

De cujus fonte lúminis
Verbi corúscant fáculæ,
Scriptúræ sacræ Núminis
Et veritátis régulæ.

Fulgens doctrínæ rádiis,
Clarus vitæ mundítia,
Splendens miris prodígiis,
Dat toti mundo gáudia.

Laus Patri sit ac Génito,
Simúlque sancto Flámini,
Qui sancti Thomæ mérito
Nos cæli jungat ágmini.
Amen.

℣. Sapiéntia requiéscit in corde suo.
℟. Et prudéntia in sermóne oris illíus.
.....
CANTICUM ZACHARIÆ.

Benedíctus Dóminus Deus Israël, * quia visitávit, et fecit redemptiónem plebis suæ:

Et eréxit cornu salútis nobis: * in domo David púeri sui.

Sicut locútus est per os sanctórum, * qui a sǽculo sunt, prophetárum ejus.

Glória Patri, et Fílio, * et Spirítui Sancto.

---

[3] The aureole is a special joy, besides that derived from the beatific vision, that some of the blessed enjoy by reason of an excelling victory they achieved by their deeds. Saint Thomas, following Catholic tradition, assigns the aureoles to virgins, martyrs, and doctors or

.....
HYMN.

From forth that fount of light
Flasheth the Word Divine,
Of Holy Writ the might,
The Church's rule and line.

With Doctor's aureole crowned,[3]
With innocency clad,
His miracles abound,
And all the earth is glad.

Praise to the Father be,
Praise to the Son and Spirit,
For Thomas' sake, may we
Heaven's company inherit.
Amen.

℣. Wisdom resteth in his heart.

℟. And prudence in the words of his lips.

.....
CANTICLE OF ZACHARIAS.

Blessed be the Lord God of Israel; * because he hath visited and wrought the redemption of his people:

And hath raised up an horn of salvation to us, * in the house of David his servant:

As he spoke by the mouth of his holy prophets, * who are from the beginning.

Glory be to the Father, and to the Son, * and to the Holy Ghost.

---

preachers. The first overcome the flesh, the second the world, the third the devil (see *Summa Theologica*, Suppl., q. 96, aa. 1, 5–7).

Sicut erat in princípio, et nunc, et semper, * et in sǽcula sæculórum. Amen.

Ant. Viror carnis flore mundítiæ, vigor vitæ fructu justítiæ, splendor verbi dono sciéntiæ, te décorant stantem in ácie, te corónant in statu glóriæ.

℣. Dómine, exáudi oratiónem meam.
℟. Et clamor meus ad te véniat.

Orémus.

Deus, qui Ecclésiam tuam beáti Thomæ, Confessóris tui atque Doctóris, mira eruditióne claríficas, et sancta operatióne fecúndas: da nobis, quǽsumus, et quæ dócuit intelléctu conspícere, et quæ egit imitatióne complére. Per Christum Dóminum nostrum. ℟. Amen.

℣. Dómine, exáudi oratiónem meam.
℟. Et clamor meus ad te véniat.
℣. Benedicámus Dómino.
℟. Deo grátias.

As it was in the beginning, is now, and ever shall be, * world without end. Amen.

Ant. The flower of purity which adorneth thy flesh, the fruits of justice which are the strength of thy life, the gift of science which giveth splendor to thy words, are thy triumph in the combat, and thy crown in the state of glory.

℣. Hear, O Lord, my prayer.
℟. And let my cry come to thee.

Let us pray.

O God, who makest thy Church glorious through the wonderful learning of blessed Thomas, thy Confessor and Doctor, and renderest her fruitful by his holy actions; grant us, we beseech thee, clearly to understand the things which he taught, and faithfully to imitate what he performed. Through Jesus Christ our Lord. ℟. Amen.

℣. Hear, O Lord, my prayer.
℟. And let my cry come to thee.
℣. Let us bless the Lord.
℟. Thanks be to God.

AD PRIMAM.

℣. Deus in adjutórium meum inténde.
℟. Dómine ad adjuvándum me festína.
Glória Patri, et Fílio, et Spirítui Sancto.
Sicut erat in princípio, et nunc, et semper, et in sǽcula sæculórum. Amen.

.....
HYMNUS.

Thomas insígnis génere,
Claram ducens oríginem,
Subit ætátis ténerae
Prædicatórum órdinem.

Laus Patri sit ac Génito,
Simúlque sancto Flámini,
Qui sancti Thomæ mérito
Nos cæli jungat ágmini.
Amen.

.....
PSALMUS LIII.

Deus in nómine tuo salvum me fac: * et in virtúte tua júdica me.

Deus exáudi oratiónem meam: * áuribus pércipe verba oris mei.

Quóniam aliéni insurrexérunt advérsum me, et fortes quæsiérunt ánimam meam: * et non proposuérunt Deum ante conspéctum suum.

AT PRIME.

℣. O God, come to my assistance.

℟. O Lord, make haste to help me.

Glory be to the Father, and to the Son, and to the Holy Ghost.

As it was in the beginning, is now, and ever shall be, world without end. Amen.

.....
HYMN.

> Our Thomas, as appears,
> Was sprung of noble stock,
> And still in tender years,
> Entered the Preachers' flock.
>
> Praise to the Father be,
> Praise to the Son and Spirit,
> For Thomas' sake, may we
> Heaven's company inherit.
> Amen.

.....
PSALM LIII.

Save me, O God, by thy name, * and judge me in thy strength.

O God, hear my prayer: * give ear to the words of my mouth.

For strangers have risen up against me; and the mighty have sought after my soul: * and they have not set God before their eyes.

Ecce enim Deus ádjuvat me: * et Dóminus suscéptor est ánimæ meæ.

Glória Patri, et Fílio, * et Spirítui Sancto.

Sicut erat in princípio, et nunc, et semper, * et in sǽcula sæculórum. Amen.

Ant. Doctor Thomas replétus grátia, præmonstrátus sacris oráculis, mundi, carnis, hostísque vítia fugat, exémplar datum sǽculis.[4]

.....
CAPITULUM. JAC. I.

Beátus vir, qui suffert tentatiónem: quóniam, cum probátus fúerit, accípiet corónam vitæ, quam repromísit Deus diligéntibus se. ℟. Deo grátias.

℟. Jesu Christe, Fili Dei vivi, * Prece Doctóris cǽlici.

Jesu Christe, Fili Dei vivi, prece Doctóris cǽlici.

℣. Tibi præsta nos gratos éffici. Prece Doctóris cǽlici.

Gloria Patri, et Fílio, et Spirítui Sancto.

Jesu Christe, Fili Dei vivi, prece Doctóris cǽlici.

---

[4] A holy hermit prophesied to Saint Thomas's mother that she would bear a son who would join the Dominicans in spite of his parents'

For behold God is my helper: * and the Lord is the protector of my soul.

Glory be to the Father, and to the Son, * and to the Holy Ghost.

As it was in the beginning, is now, and ever shall be, * world without end. Amen.

Ant. Announced beforehand by sacred oracles, Doctor Thomas is filled with grace. He flieth the snares of the world, the flesh, and the devil, and is a model to all ages to come.[4]

.....
CHAPTER. JAMES I.

Blessed is the man that endureth temptation; for when he hath been proved, he shall receive the crown of life, which God hath promised to them that love him. ℟. Thanks be to God.

℟. Jesus Christ, Son of the living God, * By the prayer of the Angelic Doctor.

Jesus Christ, Son of the living God, by the prayer of the Angelic Doctor.

℣. May we find grace before thee. By the prayer of the Angelic Doctor.

Glory be to the Father, and to the Son, and to the Holy Ghost.

Jesus Christ, Son of the living God, by the prayer of the Angelic Doctor.

---

intention that he be a monk of Monte Cassino and who would excel in sanctity and knowledge.

℣. Exsúrge, Dómine, ádjuva nos.
℟. Et líbera nos propter nomen tuum.
℣. Dómine, exáudi oratiónem meam.
℟. Et clamor meus ad te véniat.

Orémus.

Deus, qui Ecclésiam tuam beáti Thomæ, Confessóris tui atque Doctóris, mira eruditióne claríficas, et sancta operatióne fecúndas: da nobis, quæsumus, et quæ dócuit intelléctu conspícere, et quæ egit imitatióne complére. Per Christum Dóminum nostrum. ℟. Amen.

℣. Dómine, exáudi oratiónem meam.
℟. Et clamor meus ad te véniat.
℣. Benedicámus Dómino.
℟. Deo grátias.

℣. Arise, O Lord, help us.
℟. And deliver us for thy name's sake.
℣. Hear, O Lord, my prayer.
℟. And let my cry come to thee.

Let us pray.

O God, who makest thy Church glorious through the wonderful learning of blessed Thomas, thy Confessor and Doctor, and renderest her fruitful by his holy actions; grant us, we beseech thee, clearly to understand the things which he taught, and faithfully to imitate what he performed. Through Jesus Christ our Lord. ℟. Amen.

℣. Hear, O Lord, my prayer.
℟. And let my cry come to thee.
℣. Let us bless the Lord.
℟. Thanks be to God.

AD TERTIAM.

℣. Deus in adjutórium meum inténde.
℟. Dómine ad adjuvándum me festína.
Glória Patri, et Fílio, et Spirítui Sancto.
Sicut erat in princípio, et nunc, et semper, et in sǽcula sæculórum. Amen.

.....
HYMNUS.

Typum gessit lucíferi,
Splendens in cœtu núbium,
Plusquam doctóres céteri
Purgans dogma Gentílium.[5]

Laus Patri sit ac Génito,
Simúlque sancto Flámini,
Qui sancti Thomæ mérito
Nos cæli jungat ágmini.
Amen.

.....
PSALMUS XIV.

Dómine, quis habitábit in tabernáculo tuo? * aut quis requiéscet in monte sancto tuo?

Qui ingréditur sine mácula, * et operátur justítiam:

Qui lóquitur veritátem in corde suo, * qui non egit dolum in lingua sua.

---

[5] This refers to Saint Thomas's eager use of Aristotelian philosophy in the service of theology, which some of his contemporaries frowned upon.

AT TERCE.

℣. O God, come to my assistance.

℟. O Lord, make haste to help me.

Glory be to the Father, and to the Son, and to the Holy Ghost.

As it was in the beginning, is now, and ever shall be, world without end. Amen.

.....
HYMN.

> His type, the morning star,
> With light through clouds transfused,
> The arts which some would bar,
> He purified and used. [5]
>
> Praise to the Father be,
> Praise to the Son and Spirit,
> For Thomas' sake, may we
> Heaven's company inherit.
> Amen.

.....
PSALM XIV.

Lord, who shall dwell in thy tabernacle? * or who shall rest in thy holy hill?

He that walketh without blemish, * and worketh justice:

He that speaketh truth in his heart, * who hath not used deceit in his tongue.

Glória Patri, et Fílio, * et Spirítui Sancto.

Sicut erat in princípio, et nunc, et semper, * et in sǽcula sæculórum. Amen.

Ant. Mentis innocéntia flosque puritátis exstitérunt prǽvia luci veritátis.

.....
CAPITULUM. ECCLI. XLV.

Elégit eum Dóminus ex omni carne, et dedit illi coram præcépta, et legem vitæ et disciplínæ, docére Jacob testaméntum suum, et judícia sua Israël. ℟. Deo grátias.

℟. Sancte Thoma, * Audi rogántes sérvulos.
Sancte Thoma, audi rogántes sérvulos.
℣. Et impetrátam nobis cǽlitus tu defer indulgéntiam.
Audi rogántes sérvulos.
Glória Patri, et Fílio, et Spirítui Sancto.
Sancte Thoma, audi rogántes sérvulos.

℣. Pie scholárum patróne, tuórum memor óperum.
℟. Sta coram summo Júdice pro tuo cœtu páuperum.
℣. Dómine, exáudi oratiónem meam.
℟. Et clamor meus ad te véniat.

Orémus.

Deus, qui Ecclésiam tuam beáti Thomæ, Confessóris tui atque Doctóris, mira eruditióne claríficas, et

Glory be to the Father, and to the Son, * and to the Holy Ghost.

As it was in the beginning, is now, and ever shall be, * world without end. Amen.

Ant. Innocence of mind, and the flower of purity appeared first in him, and prepared the way for the light of truth.

.....

CHAPTER. ECCLUS. XLV.

The Lord chose him out of all flesh, and he gave him commandments before his face, and a law of life and instruction, that he might teach Jacob his covenant, and Israel his judgments. ℟. Thanks be to God.

℟. Saint Thomas, * Hear thy servants who pray to thee.

Saint Thomas, hear thy servants who pray to thee.

℣. And bring us from heaven the pardon thou obtainest. Hear thy servants who pray to thee.

Glory be to the Father, and to the Son, and to the Holy Ghost.

Saint Thomas, hear thy servants who pray to thee.

℣. Pious patron of schools, be mindful of thy charge.

℟. Stand before the Sovereign Judge, in behalf of thy poor servants.

℣. Hear, O Lord, my prayer.

℟. And let my cry come to thee.

Let us pray.

O God, who makest thy Church glorious through the wonderful learning of blessed Thomas, thy

sancta operatióne fecúndas: da nobis, quǽsumus, et quæ dócuit intelléctu conspícere, et quæ egit imitatióne complére. Per Christum Dóminum nostrum. ℟. Amen.

℣. Dómine, exáudi oratiónem meam.
℟. Et clamor meus ad te véniat.
℣. Benedicámus Dómino.
℟. Deo grátias.

Confessor and Doctor, and renderest her fruitful by his holy actions; grant us, we beseech thee, clearly to understand the things which he taught, and faithfully to imitate what he performed. Through Jesus Christ our Lord. ℟. Amen.

℣. Hear, O Lord, my prayer.
℟. And let my cry come to thee.
℣. Let us bless the Lord.
℟. Thanks be to God.

AD SEXTAM.

℣. Deus in adjutórium meum inténde.
℟. Dómine ad adjuvándum me festína.
Glória Patri, et Fílio, et Spirítui Sancto.
Sicut erat in princípio, et nunc, et semper, et in sǽcula sæculórum. Amen.

.....
HYMNUS.

Profúnda scrutans flúminum,
In lucem pandit ábdita,
Dum supra sensus hóminum
Obscúra facit cógnita.

Laus Patri sit ac Génito,
Simúlque sancto Flámini,
Qui sancti Thomæ mérito
Nos cæli jungat ágmini.
Amen.

.....
PSALMUS CXXX.

Dómine, non est exaltátum cor meum: * neque eláti sunt óculi mei.

Neque ambulávi in magnis: * neque in mirabílibus super me.

Si non humíliter sentiébam: * sed exaltávi ánimam meam:

Sicut ablactátus est super matre sua, * ita retribútio in ánima mea.

AT SEXT.

℣. O God, come to my assistance.
℟. O Lord, make haste to help me.
Glory be to the Father, and to the Son, and to the Holy Ghost.
As it was in the beginning, is now, and ever shall be, world without end. Amen.

.....
HYMN.

> Able the depths to scan,
> He secrets brings to light
> Above the sense of man,
> And makes the darkness bright.
>
> Praise to the Father be,
> Praise to the Son and Spirit,
> For Thomas' sake, may we
> Heaven's company inherit.
> Amen.

.....
PSALM CXXX.

Lord, my heart is not exalted: * nor are my eyes lofty.

Neither have I walked in great matters, * nor in wonderful things above me.

If I was not humbly minded, * but exalted my soul:

As a child that is weaned is towards his mother, * so reward in my soul.

Glória Patri, et Fílio, * et Spirítui Sancto.
Sicut erat in princípio, et nunc, et semper, * et in sǽcula sæculórum. Amen.
Ant. O munus Dei grátiæ, vincens quodvis miráculum! pestíferæ supérbiæ nunquam persénsit stímulum.[6]

.....
CAPITULUM. ECCLI. XXXIX.

Ipse tamquam imbres mittet elóquia sapiéntiæ suæ, et palam fáciet disciplínam doctrínæ ejus: collaudábunt multi sapiéntiam ejus, et usque in sǽculum non delébitur. ℟. Deo grátias.

℟. Pie scholárum patróne, * Tuórum memor óperum.
Pie scholárum patróne, tuórum memor óperum.
℣. Sta coram summo Júdice pro tuo cœtu páuperum. Tuórum memor óperum.
Glória Patri, et Fílio, et Spirítui Sancto.
Pie scholárum patróne, tuórum memor óperum.

℣. Magne Pater sancte Thoma, mortis hora nos tecum súscipe.
℟. Et hic semper nos pie réspice.
℣. Dómine, exáudi oratiónem meam.
℟. Et clamor meus ad te véniat.

---

[6] So great was Saint Thomas's humility that, without any loss to that virtue, he was able to testify to this gift himself, giving all the glory to God.

Glory be to the Father, and to the Son, * and to the Holy Ghost.

As it was in the beginning, is now, and ever shall be, * world without end. Amen.

Ant. O gift of divine grace, surpassing all miracles! Never did he experience the baneful influence of pride.⁶

.....

CHAPTER. ECCLUS. XXXIX.

He will pour forth the words of his wisdom as showers, and he shall shew forth the discipline he hath learned; many shall praise his wisdom, and it shall never be forgotten. ℟. Thanks be to God.

℟. Pious patron of schools, * Be mindful of thy charge.
Pious, patron of schools, be mindful of thy charge.
℣. Stand before the Sovereign Judge, in behalf of thy poor servants. Be mindful of thy charge.
Glory be to the Father, and to the Son, and to the Holy Ghost.
Pious patron of schools, be mindful of thy charge.

℣. Holy Thomas, great father, receive us to thee at the hour of our death.
℟. And look down upon us here with a favorable eye.
℣. Hear, O Lord, my prayer.
℟. And let my cry come to thee.

Orémus.

Deus, qui Ecclésiam tuam beáti Thomæ, Confessóris tui atque Doctóris, mira eruditióne claríficas, et sancta operatióne fecúndas: da nobis, quæsumus, et quæ dócuit intelléctu conspícere, et quæ egit imitatióne complére. Per Christum Dóminum nostrum. ℟. Amen.

℣. Dómine, exáudi oratiónem meam.
℟. Et clamor meus ad te véniat.
℣. Benedicámus Dómino.
℟. Deo grátias.

Let us pray.

O God, who makest thy Church glorious through the wonderful learning of blessed Thomas, thy Confessor and Doctor, and renderest her fruitful by his holy actions; grant us, we beseech thee, clearly to understand the things which he taught, and faithfully to imitate what he performed. Through Jesus Christ our Lord. ℟. Amen.

℣. Hear, O Lord, my prayer.
℟. And let my cry come to thee.
℣. Let us bless the Lord.
℟. Thanks be to God.

AD NONAM.

℣. Deus in adjutórium meum inténde.
℟. Dómine ad adjuvándum me festína.
Glória Patri, et Fílio, et Spirítui Sancto.
Sicut erat in princípio, et nunc, et semper, et in sǽcula sæculórum. Amen.

HYMNUS.

Fit paradísi flúvius
Quadripartíte pérvius:
Fit Gedeónis gládius,
Tuba, lagéna, rádius.[7]

Laus Patri sit ac Génito,
Simúlque sancto Flámini,
Qui sancti Thomæ mérito
Nos cǽli jungat ágmini.
Amen.

PSALMUS CXXVI.

Nisi Dóminus ædificáverit domum, * in vanum laboravérunt qui ædíficant eam.

Nisi Dóminus custodíerit civitátem, * frustra vígilat qui custódit eam.

Glória Patri, et Fílio, * et Spirítui Sancto.

---

[7] See Judges 7:16–22. Presumably, the trumpets and lights used by Gedeon in his victory are being used here as metaphors for the

AT NONE.

℣. O God, come to my assistance.

℟. O Lord, make haste to help me.

Glory be to the Father, and to the Son, and to the Holy Ghost.

As it was in the beginning, is now, and ever shall be, world without end. Amen.

.....
HYMN.

>River of God, he flows,
>As Eden's fourfold stream;
>As Gedeon's sword he shows,
>With trumpet, crock, and gleam.[7]
>
>Praise to the Father be,
>Praise to the Son and Spirit,
>For Thomas' sake, may we
>Heaven's company inherit.
>Amen.

.....
PSALM CXXVI.

Unless the Lord build the house, * they labour in vain that build it.

Unless the Lord keep the city, * he watcheth in vain that keepeth it.

Glory be to the Father, and to the Son, * and to the Holy Ghost.

---

preaching and teaching of Saint Thomas, by which he has triumphed over so many errors and heresies.

Sicut erat in princípio, et nunc, et semper, * et in sǽcula sæculórum. Amen.

Ant. Felix Doctor, cujus solátio Angelórum servit atténtio: Petrus, Paulus favent obséquio: Dei Mater mulcet allóquio.[8]

.....
CAPITULUM. SAP. VII.

Lætátus sum, quóniam antecedébat me ista sapiéntia: quam sine fictióne dídici, et sine invídia commúnico, et honestátem illíus non abscóndo. ℟. Deo grátias.

℟. Magne Pater sancte Thoma, * Mortis hora nos tecum súscipe.

Magne Pater sancte Thoma, mortis hora nos tecum súscipe.

℣. Et hic semper nos pie réspice. Mortis hora nos tecum súscipe.

Glória Patri, et Fílio, et Spirítui Sancto.

Magne Pater sancte Thoma, mortis hora nos tecum súscipe.

℣. Sancte Thoma, lumen Ecclésiæ.
℟. Intercéde pro nobis ad Dóminum Deum nostum.
℣. Dómine, exáudi oratiónem meam.
℟. Et clamor meus ad te véniat.

---

[8] Angels appeared to Saint Thomas to gird his loins with a cincture of purity; he also received a vision of an angel showing him a book in which his brother Reginald's name was included amongst the martyrs because he died under Emperor Frederick II for his fidelity to the Church. Saints Peter and Paul appeared to Saint Thomas after

As it was in the beginning, is now, and ever shall be, * world without end. Amen.

Ant. Happy Doctor: the attention of angels ministereth to his comfort; Peter and Paul assist him with their good offices; the Mother of God favoreth him with her sweet conversation.[8]

.....

CHAPTER. WISDOM VII.

I rejoiced: for this wisdom went before me, which I have learned without guile, and communicate without envy, and her riches I hide not. ℟. Thanks be to God.

℟. Holy Thomas, great father, * Receive us to thee at the hour of our death.

Holy Thomas, great father, receive us to thee at the hour of our death.

℣. And look down upon us here with a favorable eye. Receive us to thee at the hour of our death.

Glory be to the Father, and to the Son, and to the Holy Ghost.

Holy Thomas, great father, receive us to thee at the hour of our death.

℣. Saint Thomas, light of the Church.
℟. Intercede for us with the Lord our God.
℣. Hear, O Lord, my prayer.
℟. And let my cry come to thee.

---

he prayed for help in understanding a passage of Isaias. Our Lady appeared to him to affirm the holiness of his life and the truth of his teaching, and to tell him that "he had obtained whatever he had asked of God through her with deliberation," including that he would remain a simple friar (William of Tocco, "Vita," ch. 32).

Orémus.

Deus, qui Ecclésiam tuam beáti Thomæ, Confessóris tui atque Doctóris, mira eruditióne claríficas, et sancta operatióne fecúndas: da nobis, quǽsumus, et quæ dócuit intelléctu conspícere, et quæ egit imitatióne complére. Per Christum Dóminum nostrum. ℟. Amen.

℣. Dómine, exáudi oratiónem meam.
℟. Et clamor meus ad te véniat.
℣. Benedicámus Dómino.
℟. Deo grátias.

Let us pray.

O God, who makest thy Church glorious through the wonderful learning of blessed Thomas, thy Confessor and Doctor, and renderest her fruitful by his holy actions; grant us, we beseech thee, clearly to understand the things which he taught, and faithfully to imitate what he performed. Through Jesus Christ our Lord. ℟. Amen.

℣. Hear, O Lord, my prayer.
℟. And let my cry come to thee.
℣. Let us bless the Lord.
℟. Thanks be to God.

AD VESPERAS.

℣. Deus in adjutórium meum inténde.
℟. Dómine ad adjuvándum me festína.
Glória Patri, et Fílio, et Spirítui Sancto.
Sicut erat in princípio, et nunc, et semper, et in sǽcula sæculórum. Amen.

PSALMUS CXI.

Beátus vir, qui timet Dóminum: * in mandátis ejus volet nimis.

Potens in terra erit semen ejus: * generátio rectórum benedicétur.

Glória, et divítiæ in domo ejus: * et justítia ejus manet in sǽculum sǽculi.

Glória Patri, et Fílio, * et Spirítui Sancto.

Sicut erat in princípio, et nunc, et semper, * et in sǽcula sæculórum. Amen.

Ant. Qui timet Dóminum, in mandátis ejus cupit nimis.

CAPITULUM. ECCLI. XLV.

Elégit eum Dóminus ex omni carne, et dedit illi coram præcépta, et legem vitæ et disciplínæ, docére Jacob testaméntum suum, et judícia sua Israël.
℟. Deo grátias.

AT VESPERS.

℣. O God, come to my assistance.

℟. O Lord, make haste to help me.

Glory be to the Father, and to the Son, and to the Holy Ghost.

As it was in the beginning, is now, and ever shall be, world without end. Amen.

PSALM CXI.

Blessed is the man that feareth the Lord: * he shall delight exceedingly in his commandments.

His seed shall be mighty upon earth: * the generation of the righteous shall be blessed.

Glory and wealth shall be in his house: * and his justice remaineth for ever and ever.

Glory be to the Father, and to the Son, * and to the Holy Ghost.

As it was in the beginning, is now, and ever shall be, * world without end. Amen.

Ant. He that feareth the Lord shall delight exceedingly in his commandments.

CHAPTER. ECCLUS. XLV.

The Lord chose him out of all flesh, and he gave him commandments before his face, and a law of life and instruction, that he might teach Jacob his covenant, and Israel his judgments. ℟. Thanks be to God.

.....
HYMNUS.

Lauda, mater Ecclésia,
Thomæ felícem éxitum,
Qui pervénit ad gáudia
Per verbi vitæ méritum.

Fossa Nova tunc súscipit
Thecam thesáuri grátiæ,
Cum Christus Thomam éfficit
Herédem regni glóriæ.[9]

Laus Patri sit ac Génito,
Simúlque sancto Flámini,
Qui sancti Thomæ mérito
Nos cæli jungat ágmini.
Amen.

℣. Ora pro nobis beáte Thoma.
℟. Ut digni efficiámur promissiónibus Christi.

.....
CANTICUM BEATÆ MARIÆ VIRGINIS.

Magníficat * ánima mea Dóminum:
Et exsultávit spíritus meus * in Deo salutári meo.
   Quia respéxit humilitátem ancíllæ suæ: * ecce enim ex hoc beátam me dicent omnes generatiónes.
   Glória Patri, et Fílio, * et Spirítui Sancto.

---

[9] Fossa Nova is the name of the Cistercian monastery where Saint Thomas died whilst on his way to the Second Council of Lyons at the command of Blessed Gregory X.

HYMN.

O Mother Church, attest
Thy servant's happy end,
Who by God's Word is blest
With joys all else transcend.

See Fossa Nova take
The treasure casket rare
Of grace, when Christ doth make
Thomas his Kingdom's heir.[9]

Praise to the Father be,
Praise to the Son and Spirit,
For Thomas' sake, may we
Heaven's company inherit.
Amen.

℣. Pray for us, O blessed Thomas.

℟. That we may be made worthy of the promises of Christ.

CANTICLE OF THE BLESSED VIRGIN MARY.

My soul * doth magnify the Lord.

And my spirit hath rejoiced * in God my Saviour.

Because he hath regarded the humility of his handmaid; * for behold from henceforth all generations shall call me blessed.

Glory be to the Father, and to the Son, * and to the Holy Ghost.

Sicut erat in princípio, et nunc, et semper, * et in sǽcula sæculórum. Amen.

Ant. O Thoma, laus et glória Prædicatórum órdinis, nos transfer ad cæléstia, proféssor sacri Núminis.

℣. Dómine, exáudi oratiónem meam.
℟. Et clamor meus ad te véniat.

Orémus.

Deus, qui Ecclésiam tuam beáti Thomæ, Confessóris tui atque Doctóris, mira eruditióne claríficas, et sancta operatióne fecúndas: da nobis, quǽsumus, et quæ dócuit intelléctu conspícere, et quæ egit imitatióne complére. Per Christum Dóminum nostrum. ℟. Amen.

℣. Dómine, exáudi oratiónem meam.
℟. Et clamor meus ad te véniat.
℣. Benedicámus Dómino.
℟. Deo grátias.

As it was in the beginning, is now, and ever shall be, * world without end. Amen.

Ant. O Thomas, honor and glory of the Order of Preachers, transport us to the celestial regions, herald of the Divinity.

℣. Hear, O Lord, my prayer.
℟. And let my cry come to thee.

Let us pray.

O God, who makest thy Church glorious through the wonderful learning of blessed Thomas, thy Confessor and Doctor, and renderest her fruitful by his holy actions; grant us, we beseech thee, clearly to understand the things which he taught, and faithfully to imitate what he performed. Through Jesus Christ our Lord. ℟. Amen.

℣. Hear, O Lord, my prayer.
℟. And let my cry come to thee.
℣. Let us bless the Lord.
℟. Thanks be to God.

AD COMPLETORIUM.

℣. Deus in adjutórium meum inténde.
℟. Dómine ad adjuvándum me festína.
Glória Patri, et Fílio, et Spirítui Sancto.
Sicut erat in princípio, et nunc, et semper, et in sǽcula sæculórum. Amen.

PSALMUS CXXXIII.

Ecce nunc benedícite Dóminum, * omnes servi Dómini:

Qui statis in domo Dómini, * in átriis domus Dei nostri.

Glória Patri, et Fílio, * et Spirítui Sancto.

Sicut erat in princípio, et nunc, et semper, * et in sǽcula sæculórum. Amen.

Ant. Liber carnis vínculo cælum introívit, ubi pleno póculo gustat quod sitívit.

CAPITULUM. ECCLI. XV.

In médio Ecclésiæ apéruit os ejus, et implévit eum Dóminus spíritu sapiéntiæ et intelléctus: stolam glóriæ índuit eum. ℟. Deo grátias.

AT COMPLINE.

℣. O God, come to my assistance.

℟. O Lord, make haste to help me.

Glory be to the Father, and to the Son, and to the Holy Ghost.

As it was in the beginning, is now, and ever shall be, world without end. Amen.

.....
PSALM CXXXIII.

Behold now bless ye the Lord, * all ye servants of the Lord:

Who stand in the house of the Lord, * in the courts of the house of our God.

Glory be to the Father, and to the Son, * and to the Holy Ghost.

As it was in the beginning, is now, and ever shall be, * world without end. Amen.

Ant. Free from the bonds of the flesh, he entered heaven, where he drinketh the fulness of the torrent for which he thirsted.

.....
CHAPTER. ECCLUS. XV.

In the midst of the church the Lord hath opened his mouth, and hath filled him with the spirit of wisdom and understanding; he hath clothed him with a robe of glory. ℟. Thanks be to God.

HYMNUS.

Manens doctrínæ véritas,
Et fúneris intégritas,
Mira fragrans suávitas,
Ægris colláta sánitas

Monstrat hunc dignum láudibus[10]
Terræ, ponto, et súperis:
Nos juvet suis précibus,
Deo comméndet méritis.

Laus Patri sit ac Génito,
Simúlque sancto Flámini,
Qui sancti Thomæ mérito
Nos cæli jungat ágmini.
Amen.

℣. Custódi nos, beáte Thoma, ut pupíllam óculi.
℟. Sub umbra alárum tuárum prótege nos.

CANTICUM SIMEONIS.

Nunc dimíttis servum tuum Dómine, * secúndum verbum tuum in pace:
Quia vidérunt óculi mei * salutáre tuum,
Quod parásti * ante fáciem ómnium populórum:
Lumen ad revelatiónem géntium, * et glóriam plebis tuæ Israël.
Glória Patri, et Fílio, * et Spirítui Sancto.

---

[10] Later versions (e.g., 1947) of the OP Breviary have *Monstrant* here, but the older ones (e.g., 1909) have *Monstrat*, so the original form has been let to stand, since it is not erroneous.

HYMN.

His doctrine ever true,
His uncorrupted frame,
Exhaling fragrance rare
To heal the sick and maim,

Approve him worthy praise
In earth, and sea, and sky;
May he uplift always
Our souls to God on high.

Praise to the Father be,
Praise to the Son and Spirit,
For Thomas' sake, may we
Heaven's company inherit.
Amen.

℣. Keep us, blessed Thomas, as the apple of thy eye.
℟. Protect us under the shadow of thy wings.

CANTICLE OF SIMEON.

Now thou dost dismiss thy servant, O Lord, * according to thy word in peace;

Because my eyes have seen * thy salvation,

Which thou hast prepared * before the face of all peoples:

A light to the revelation of the Gentiles, * and the glory of thy people Israel.

Glory be to the Father, and to the Son, * and to the Holy Ghost.

Sicut erat in princípio, et nunc, et semper, * et in sǽcula sæculórum. Amen.

Ant. O spéculum mundítiæ, carnis carens spurcítiis, tuæ coléntes hódie felicitátis gáudia, transfer ad regnum glóriæ, post hujus vitæ stádia.

℣. Dómine, exáudi oratiónem meam.
℟. Et clamor meus ad te véniat.

Orémus.

Deus, qui Ecclésiam tuam beáti Thomæ, Confessóris tui atque Doctóris, mira eruditióne claríficas, et sancta operatióne fecúndas: da nobis, quǽsumus, et quæ dócuit intelléctu conspícere, et quæ egit imitatióne complére. Per Christum Dóminum nostrum. ℟. Amen.

℣. Dómine, exáudi oratiónem meam.
℟. Et clamor meus ad te véniat.
℣. Benedicámus Dómino.
℟. Deo grátias.

As it was in the beginning, is now, and ever shall be, * world without end. Amen.

Ant. O mirror of purity, disengaged from all impediments of the flesh, we celebrate on this day the joys of thy felicity; transfer us, after this life hath passed away, to the kingdom of glory.

℣. Hear, O Lord, my prayer.
℟. And let my cry come to thee.

Let us pray.

O God, who makest thy Church glorious through the wonderful learning of blessed Thomas, thy Confessor and Doctor, and renderest her fruitful by his holy actions; grant us, we beseech thee, clearly to understand the things which he taught, and faithfully to imitate what he performed. Through Jesus Christ our Lord. ℟. Amen.

℣. Hear, O Lord, my prayer.
℟. And let my cry come to thee.
℣. Let us bless the Lord.
℟. Thanks be to God.

ANTIPHONÆ ET RESPONSORIA EX OFFICIO SANCTI THOMÆ AQUINATIS

FELIX THOMAS, DOCTOR ECCLÉSIÆ, LUMEN mundi, splendor Itáliæ, candens virgo flore mundítiæ, bina gaudet coróna glóriæ. (*Super Psalmos Antiphona ad I Vesperas.*)[1]

Scandit Doctor civis cæléstium, orbis decor, dux, lux fidélium, norma, limes, lex morum ómnium, vas virtútum ad vitæ brávium. (*Ad Magnificat Antiphona ad I Vesperas, die 7 Martii; in aliis festis, Antiphona* O THOMA, *ut in Officio Parvo ad Vesperas.*)

Adsunt Doctóris cǽlici Thomæ festa solémnia: Devotióne súpplici laudes promat Ecclésia. (*Invitatorium.*)

(*Antiphona prima ad Matutinum* DOCTOR THOMAS, *ut in Officio Parvo ad Primam; secunda* MENTIS INNOCÉNTIA, *ut in Officio Parvo ad Tertiam.*)

Ope Doctóris cǽlici tota gaudet Ecclésia: fulget ordo Domínici peculiári glória. (*Antiphona tertia ad Matutinum.*)

ANTIPHONS AND RESPONSORIES FROM THE OFFICE OF SAINT THOMAS AQUINAS

BLESSED THOMAS, DOCTOR OF THE CHURCH, light of the world, splendor of Italy, a virgin shining with the flower of purity, rejoiceth in his twofold crown of glory. (Psalm antiphon at First Vespers.)[1]

The holy Doctor, a citizen of the heavenly courts, the splendor of the world, the guide and light of the faithful, a pattern, path, and law of all morality, a vessel of virtues, ascendeth to the prize of eternal life. (*Magnificat antiphon at First Vespers for his principal feast; on the other feasts, the Antiphon* O THOMAS, *as in the Little Office at Vespers, is used.*)

The solemn feast of the heavenly Doctor Thomas hath arrived: let the Church pour forth praises with humble devotion. (Invitatory.)

(*The first antiphon at Matins is* ANNOUNCED BEFOREHAND, *as in the Little Office at Prime; the second is* INNOCENCE OF MIND, *as in the Little Office at Terce.*)

The whole Church rejoiceth in the aid of the heavenly Doctor; the Order of Saint Dominic shineth forth with especial glory. (*Third antiphon at Matins.*)

---

[1] The "twofold crown" refers to the aureoles Saint Thomas received as virgin and doctor.

(*Antiphona quarta ad Matutinum* O MUNUS DEI GRÁTIÆ, *ut in Officio Parvo ad Sextam.*)

Prece curat sócium febrem patiéntem, et in ora véstium sánguine fluéntem. (*Antiphona quinta ad Matutinum.*)[2]

Stella candens émicat, stupórem dans insólitum: quæ instántem índicat beáti Thomæ tránsitum. (*Antiphona sexta ad Matutinum.*)[3]

Instánte vitæ término, vidit regna cæléstia: et reveránte Dómino, novit paráta præmia. (*Antiphona septima ad Matutinum.*)[4]

Semenávit hic lárgiter Doctor virtuósus: metit illic felíciter victor gloriósus. (*Antiphona octava ad Matutinum.*)

Sidus de nube tráhitur, de fœno flos elícitur, salque de terra tóllitur, dum Thomas cælo rédditur. (*Antiphona nona ad Matutinum.*)

Adest dies lætítiæ, quo Thomas Doctor ínclytus fit civis cæli cúriæ, bina coróna præditus. (*Antiphona prima ad Laudes et Super Psalmos Antiphona ad II Vesperas, die 7 Martii;*

---

[2] A *socius* was the name given in the Dominican Order to a friar who served a role similar to that of a secretary. Saint Thomas's *socius* was Reginald of Piperno, whom he healed by prayer and the application of a relic of Saint Agnes, to whom Saint Thomas had a great devotion. The second miracle occurred when, after Saint Thomas had preached at Saint Peter's on Easter Sunday, a woman touched the hem of his cappa and was cured of her issue of blood.

(*The fourth antiphon at Matins is* O GIFT OF DIVINE GRACE, *as in the Little Office at Sext.*)

By his prayer he healeth his *socius* afflicted with a fever and, by the hem of his cloak, a woman troubled with an issue of blood. (*Fifth antiphon at Matins.*)[2]

A radiant star shineth forth, causing unwonted wonder, and maketh known that the passing of blessed Thomas draweth nigh. (*Sixth antiphon at Matins.*)[3]

As the end of his life drew nigh, he saw the heavenly kingdom; and by the Lord's revelation, he learned of the rewards prepared for him. (*Seventh antiphon at Matins.*)[4]

The virtuous Doctor sowed bountifully here below; in heaven, triumphant in glory, he joyfully reapeth his reward. (*Eighth antiphon at Matins.*)

A star is drawn from the clouds, a flower from the straw, and salt is taken from the earth when Thomas is yielded to heaven. (*Ninth antiphon at Matins.*)

The day of joy hath arrived, on which the glorious Doctor Thomas is made a citizen of the heavenly courts, adorned with a twofold crown. (*First antiphon at Lauds*

---

[3] When Saint Thomas was ill at Naples, a star was seen to enter through the window and hover above his head. On the three days before his death, a star like a comet appeared above the monastery of Fossa Nova and disappeared once he had died.

[4] A few months before his death, Saint Thomas heard Our Lord speaking from the Crucifix. Christ approved his doctrine and asked him what reward he would have in return. Saint Thomas asked for none other than Christ himself.

in aliis festis, Antiphona COLLAUDÉTUR CHRISTUS, *ut in Officio Parvo ad Laudes.*)

Aurum sub terra tégitur, et lucérna sub módio: sed virtus Dei cérnitur miraculórum rádio. (*Antiphona secunda ad Laudes.*)

Alma mater Ecclésia, Christi fundáta sánguine, sceptra conscéndit grándia, novi Doctóris lúmine. (*Antiphona tertia ad Laudes.*)

Pressus vi dæmónii cito liberátur: raptu mersus flúvii vitæ restaurátur. (*Antiphona quarta ad Laudes.*)

Tumor gulæ péllitur, leprósus mundátur, cæco lumen rédditur, claudo gressus datur. (*Antiphona quinta ad Laudes.*)

(*Ad Benedictus Antiphona* VIROR CARNIS, *ut in Officio Parvo ad Laudes.*)

Militántis Doctor Ecclésiæ, virgináli florens mundítia, triumphántis optáta cúriæ, sancte Thoma, largíre gáudia. (*Ad Magnificat Antiphona ad II Vesperas.*)

℟. Sancti viri verbum prophéticum præmonstrávit mundo miríficum sanctum Thomam Doctórem cǽlicum, * Sectatúrum sanctum Domínicum. ℣. Nam

and Psalm antiphon at Second Vespers for his principal feast; on the other feasts, the antiphon MAY CHRIST THE KING OF GLORY, *as in the Little Office at Lauds, is used.*)

Gold is hidden beneath the earth and a candle under a bushel; but the power of God is revealed by the light of his miracles. (*Second antiphon at Lauds.*)

Nourishing Mother Church, founded by the blood of Christ, embarketh on her great dominion by the light of a new Doctor. (*Third antiphon at Lauds.*)[5]

A man oppressed by demon's might is quickly delivered; a man drowned by the force of a river is restored to life. (*Fourth antiphon at Lauds.*)

A tumor of the throat is healed, a leper is cleansed, light is restored to a blind man, a lame man walketh again. (*Fifth antiphon at Lauds.*)

(*The Benedictus antiphon is* THE FLOWER OF PURITY, *as in the Little Office.*)

Doctor of the Church militant, flowering with virginal purity, grant, O Saint Thomas, the hoped-for joys of the triumphant court of heaven. (*Magnificat antiphon at Second Vespers.*)

℟. The prophetic word of the holy man foretold to the world the wondrous Saint Thomas, the heavenly Doctor, * A follower of Saint Dominic. ℣. For the holy

---

[5] Or this could be rendered: Beloved Mother Church, founded by the blood of Christ, ascendeth to lofty heights by the light of a new Doctor.

vir sanctus hunc matri grávidæ ducem prompsit doctrínæ lúcidæ. — Sectatúrum sanctum Domínicum. (*Responsorium primum.*)

℟. Christi pia tractus dulcédine, mundum linquens probátur túrbine: * Pugil fortis raptus de órdine, vicit prorsus pulsa libídine. ℣. Orat pressa cruce mirífica: renes cingit manus angélica. — Pugil fortis raptus de órdine, vicit prorsus pulsa libídine. (*Responsorium secundum.*)[6]

℟. O ánima sanctíssima, qua contempláne dúlciter, corpus linquébat ínfima, * Stans sursum mirabíliter. ℣. Nullo prorsus fultus subsídio, levabátur in raptus gáudio. — Stans sursum mirabíliter. — Glória Patri, et Fílio, et Spirítui Sancto. — Stans sursum mirabíliter. (*Responsorium tertium.*)

(*Responsorium quartum* DE EXCÉLSIS, *ut in Officio Parvo.*)

℟. Felix Doctor, cujus solátio Angelórum servit atténtio: Petrus, Paulus favent obséquio: * Dei Mater mulcet allóquio. ℣. Elevátus a terra cérnitur, Crucifíxus eum allóquitur. — Dei Mater mulcet allóquio. (*Responsorium quintum.*)

---

[6] This refers to the famous incident where Saint Thomas overcame his brothers' perverse attempt to make him leave the Dominicans. He marked a cross on the wall and prayed for God's protection of his purity. He received a vision of two angels who girded his loins and promised he would ever preserve his purity.

man disclosed to his expectant mother that he would be a guide of luminous teaching. — A follower of Saint Dominic. (*First responsory.*)

℟. Drawn by the holy sweetness of Christ, he forsaketh the world and is proved by a violent trial: * A strong athlete snatched from his Order, he conquered, utterly repelling lust. ℣. He prayeth before the wondrous cross he drew; the hands of angels gird his loins. — A strong athlete snatched from his Order, he conquered, utterly repelling lust. (*Second responsory.*)[6]

℟. O most holy soul, in the sweetness of whose contemplation the body was raised from the earth, * Resting miraculously suspended. ℣. Without any support, he was raised from the earth in a rapture of joy. — Resting miraculously suspended. — Glory be to the Father, and to the Son, and to the Holy Ghost. — Resting miraculously suspended. (*Third responsory.*)

(*The fourth responsory is* DESCENDING FROM HEAVEN, *as in the Little Office.*)

℟. Happy Doctor: the attention of angels ministereth to his comfort; Peter and Paul assist him with their good offices; * The Mother of God favoreth him with her sweet conversation. ℣. He is seen elevated above the earth; the Crucified converseth with him. — The Mother of God favoreth him with her sweet conversation. (*Fifth responsory.*)

℟. Sidus missum Thomæ de súperis, novo signo divíni múneris, * Hunc cæléstem demónstrat céteris, Verbo, vita, doctrína, lítteris. ℣. Quam excélsus, quem cæli prædicant: quam præclárus, quem stellæ índicant! — Hunc cæléstem demónstrat céteris, verbo, vita, doctrína, lítteris. — Glória Patri, et Fílio, et Spirítui Sancto. — Verbo, vita, doctrína, lítteris. (*Responsorium sextum.*)

℟. Scholas Thomæ Paulus ingréditur, sacra simul fantur mystéria: digne tandem per raptum tráhitur * Vir cæléstis ad cæli præmia. ℣. Clamor Fratris trinus emíttitur: Doctor noster a nobis tóllitur. — Vir cæléstis ad cæli præmia. (*Responsorium septimum.*)[7]

℟. Beáti Thomæ glória divo fulsit miráculo, dum odóris fragrántia mira fluxit ex túmulo: * Qui nitens pudicítia, vixit absque piáculo. ℣. Hic speciáli grátia, lustráto mentis óculo, celsa novit mystéria, cæli doctus oráculo. — Qui nitens pudicítia, vixit absque piáculo. (*Responsorium octavum.*)

(*Responsorium nonum* SERTUM GESTANS, *ut in Officio Parvo.*)

---

[7] Friar Paul of Aquila had a vision in Naples at the time of Saint Thomas's death: he saw the Angelic Doctor lecturing, then Saint Paul the Apostle, to whom he had a great devotion, entered and affirmed that he had correctly expounded his epistles. He then led

℟. A star is sent to Thomas from heaven by a new sign of the divine favor; * It showeth to others that he is heavenly In his words, his life, his teaching, and his writings. ℣. O how eminent is this man whom the heavens praise, how illustrious is he whom the stars proclaim! —It showeth to others that he is heavenly in his words, his life, his teaching, and his writings. —Glory be to the Father, and to the Son, and to the Holy Ghost. —In his words, his life, his teaching, and his writings. (*Sixth responsory.*)

℟. Paul entereth Thomas's school, and they speak together of the sacred mysteries; at length he is worthily drawn away, snatched from the earth, * A heavenly man to the rewards of heaven. ℣. Thrice a Friar crieth out: Our teacher is taken from us. —A heavenly man to the rewards of heaven. (*Seventh responsory.*)[7]

℟. The glory of blessed Thomas shone forth with a divine miracle when a wondrous fragrance flowed from his tomb. * Radiant with purity, he lived without sin. ℣. By a special grace, his mind's eye illumined, he learned the lofty mysteries, taught by heavenly revelation. —Radiant with purity, he lived without sin. (*Eighth responsory.*)

(*The ninth responsory is* HE WAS SEEN, *as in the Little Office.*)

Saint Thomas out to take him to a place where he would receive "a clearer understanding of all things" (Tocco, "Vita," ch. 60). This vision caused the friar to cry out as described in the responsory.

ORATIO CONFRATERNITATIS MILITIÆ ANGELICÆ

O CANDÓRIS LÍLIUM ELÉCTUM, SANCTE Thoma puríssime, qui baptísmi stolam júgiter illibátam asservásti; qui a duóbus Angelis præcínctus, vere Angelus in carne fuísti: Jesu Agno sine mácula et Maríæ vírginum Regínæ, me, quæso, comménda; ut, et ego sacrum tuæ victóriæ advérsus carnem signum mecum déferens, ejúsdem puritátis párticeps tuíque imitátor exístens in terra, tecum tandem, o meæ puritátis alme defénsor, inter Angelos coróner in cælis.

Pater, Ave, Glória Patri.

℣. Ora pro nobis beáte Thoma.
℟. Ut digni efficiámur promissiónibus Christi.

Orémus.

Deus, qui nos in duríssimo castitátis certámine constitútos almo sancti Thomæ cíngulo (vel numísmate) muníre dignátus es, largíre supplícibus tuis, ita cælésti ejus subsídio lascívum córporis et ánimæ hostem in hac milítia felíciter superáre, ut perpétuæ puritátis lílio coronáti inter castas Angelórum ácies beatitúdinis palmam a te recípere mereámur. Per Christum Dóminum nostrum. ℟. Amen.

PRAYER OF THE ANGELIC WARFARE CONFRATERNITY

CHOSEN LILY OF INNOCENCE, MOST CHASTE Saint Thomas, thou who didst ever preserve thy baptismal robe unspotted, thou who wast by two angels girded, thou who wast thyself a true angel in the flesh, I intreat thee to recommend me to Jesus, the spotless Lamb, and to Mary, the Queen of Virgins, that wearing around my loins thy holy girdle which was granted thee as a pledge of thy purity, and imitating thy virtues upon earth, I may one day be crowned with thee, O thou powerful protector of my innocence!

Our Father. Hail Mary. Glory be to the Father.

℣. Pray for us, O blessed Thomas.

℟. That we may be made worthy of the promises of Christ.

Let us pray.

O God, who didst deign to arm us with the girdle (or medal) of Saint Thomas in the assaults made upon our innocence, grant to our earnest prayers that we, under his heavenly protection, the impure enemy of our body and soul in this warfare may happily overcome; and adorned with the unfading lily of purity, in the midst of the angelic host, may receive the palm of celestial bliss. Through Christ our Lord. ℟. Amen.

ORATIONES AD SANCTUM THOMAM, PATRONUM SCHOLARUM CATHOLICARUM

DOCTOR ANGÉLICE SANCTE THOMA, THEOlogórum princeps et philosophórum norma, præclárum christiáni orbis decus et Ecclésiæ lumen, scholárum ómnium catholicárum cæléstis patróne, qui sapiéntiam sine fictióne didicísti et sine invídia commúnicas, ipsam Sapiéntiam Fílium Dei deprecáre pro nobis, ut veniénte in nos Spíritu sapiéntiæ, ea quæ docuísti intéllectu conspiciámus, et quæ egísti imitatióne compleámus; doctrínæ et virtútis, quibus in terris solis instar semper eluxísti, partícipes efficiámur; ac tandem eárum suavíssimis frúctibus perénniter tecum delectémur in cælis, divínam Sapiéntiam collaudántes per infiníta sǽcula sæculórum. ℟. Amen.

O sancte Thoma, scholárum patróne, fidem invíctam, caritátem férvidam, vitam castíssimam, sciéntiam veram a Deo nobis óbtine per Christum Dóminum nostrum. ℟. Amen.

PRAYERS TO SAINT THOMAS, PATRON OF CATHOLIC SCHOOLS

ANGELIC DOCTOR, SAINT THOMAS, PRINCE of theologians and model of philosophers, bright ornament of the Christian world, light of the Church and patron of all Catholic schools, who didst learn wisdom without guile and dost communicate it without envy, pray for us to the Son of God who is Wisdom itself, that, by the coming of the Spirit of Wisdom upon us, we may clearly understand that which thou didst teach, and, by imitating thee, may bring to completion that which thou didst do; that we may be made partakers both of thy doctrine and thy holiness, whereby thou didst shine on earth even as the sun; and finally that we may enjoy with thee in heaven for evermore the most delectable fruits of the same, praising together with thee divine Wisdom through endless ages. ℟. Amen.

O Saint Thomas, patron of schools, obtain for us from God an unconquered faith, fervent charity, a most chaste life, and true knowledge. Through Christ our Lord. ℟. Amen.

ORATIO ANTE STUDIUM SANCTI THOMÆ

Verbum Dei, verba nostra confórma.
Spíritus Dei, corda nostra inflámma.
Deus illuminátio nostra,
Angelíque custódes,
méntium nostrárum lúmina corroboráte,
phantásmata nostra ordináte et illustráte,
et nos ad diligéntem consideratiónem excitáte.
Sancte Thoma Aquínas, Doctor Angélice, ora pro nobis,
ádjuva nos ut quæ scripsísti intelligámus.

PRAYER BEFORE STUDYING SAINT THOMAS[1]

Word of God, form our words.
Spirit of God, inflame our hearts.
God our enlightenment,
Guardian angels,
strengthen the lights of our minds,
order and illumine our images,
and arouse us to consider more carefully.
Saint Thomas Aquinas, Angelic Doctor, pray for us;
help us to understand what you have written.

---

[1] This prayer was always used by Duane Berquist (1936–2019), a beloved teacher whose knowledge of Aristotle, Saint Thomas Aquinas, and Shakespeare was legendary. The prayer is probably his own composition. The Latin version was prepared by Gerhard Eger and Zachary Thomas.

LITANIÆ IN HONOREM SANCTI THOMÆ AQUINATIS, ECCLESIÆ DOCTORIS, ET CASTITATIS PATRONI
(*Ad usum privatum*)

ýrie eléison.
Christe eléison.
Kýrie eléison.
Christe audi nos.
Christe exáudi nos.
Pater de cælis Deus, *miserére nobis.*
Fili Redémptor mundi Deus, *miserére nobis.*
Spiritus Sancte Deus, *miserére nobis.*
Sancta Trínitas unus Deus, *miserére nobis.*
Sancta María, *ora pro nobis.*
Sancta Dei Génitrix, *ora pro nobis.*
Sancta Virgo vírginum, *ora pro nobis.*
Sancte Thoma, *ora pro nobis.*
Sancte Thoma, Doctor Angélice, *ora pro nobis.*
Sancte Thoma, nóbilis génere, virtúte nobílior, *ora pro nobis.*
Sancte Thoma, vanitátes mundi generóso ánimo contémnens, *ora pro nobis.*
Sancte Thoma, voci Dei, in eligéndo vitæ statu, prompte obédiens, *ora pro nobis.*
Sancte Thoma, nec minis nec promíssis a sancto propósito avocáte, *ora pro nobis.*

LITANY IN HONOR OF SAINT THOMAS AQUINAS, DOCTOR OF THE CHURCH AND PATRON OF CHASTITY

(For private use)

Lord, have mercy on us.
Christ, have mercy on us.
Lord, have mercy on us.
Christ, hear us.
Christ, graciously hear us.
God the Father of Heaven, *have mercy on us.*
God the Son, Redeemer of the world, *have mercy on us.*
God the Holy Ghost, *have mercy on us.*
Holy Trinity, one God, *have mercy on us.*
Holy Mary, *pray for us.*
Holy Mother of God, *pray for us.*
Holy Virgin of virgins, *pray for us.*
Saint Thomas, *pray for us.*
Saint Thomas, Angelic Doctor, *pray for us.*
Saint Thomas, noble by birth, yet more noble by virtue, *pray for us.*
Saint Thomas, who didst despise the vanities of the world with a generous heart, *pray for us.*
Saint Thomas, who didst promptly obey the voice of God in choosing thy state in life, *pray for us.*
Saint Thomas, whom neither threats nor promises could draw away from thy holy undertaking, *pray for us.*

Sancte Thoma, persecutiónes fratrum tuórum cum gáudio sústinens, *ora pro nobis.*
Sancte Thoma, digníssime fili sancti Patris Domínici, *ora pro nobis.*
Sancte Thoma, decus órdinis Prædicatórum, *ora pro nobis.*
Sancte Thoma, spéculum humilitátis, *ora pro nobis.*
Sancte Thoma, exémplar obediéntiæ, *ora pro nobis.*
Sancte Thoma, forma pœniténtiæ, *ora pro nobis.*
Sancte Thoma, oratióni et contemplatióni addictíssime, *ora pro nobis.*
Sancte Thoma, magíster perfectiónis, *ora pro nobis.*
Sancte Thoma, castitátis amátor exími, *ora pro nobis.*
Sancte Thoma, castitátis cíngulo ab Angelis præcíncte, *ora pro nobis.*
Sancte Thoma, castitátis patrónus ab Ecclésia constitúte, *ora pro nobis.*
Sancte Thoma, zelo fídei exardéscens, *ora pro nobis.*
Sancte Thoma, prædicátor veritátis, *ora pro nobis.*
Sancte Thoma, potens in ópere et sermóne, *ora pro nobis.*
Sancte Thoma, sal terræ, *ora pro nobis.*
Sancte Thoma, lux mundi fulgidíssima, *ora pro nobis.*
Sancte Thoma, cólumen Ecclésiæ firmíssimum, *ora pro nobis.*
Sancte Thoma, sápiens, sicut habet sapiéntiam Angelus Dei, *ora pro nobis.*
Sancte Thoma, confutátor irrefragábilis hæreticórum, *ora pro nobis.*
Sancte Thoma, explanátor doctíssime mysteriórum, *ora pro nobis.*

Saint Thomas, who didst endure with joy the persecutions of thy brethren, *pray for us.*
Saint Thomas, most worthy son of the holy Father Dominic, *pray for us.*
Saint Thomas, glory of the Order of Preachers, *pray for us.*
Saint Thomas, mirror of humility, *pray for us.*
Saint Thomas, exemplar of obedience, *pray for us.*
Saint Thomas, pattern of penance, *pray for us.*
Saint Thomas, most dedicated to prayer and contemplation, *pray for us.*
Saint Thomas, master of perfection, *pray for us.*
Saint Thomas, distinguished lover of chastity, *pray for us.*
Saint Thomas, girded by angels with the cincture of chastity, *pray for us.*
Saint Thomas, declared patron of chastity by the Church, *pray for us.*
Saint Thomas, enflamed with zeal for the Faith, *pray for us.*
Saint Thomas, preacher of the truth, *pray for us.*
Saint Thomas, mighty in work and word, *pray for us.*
Saint Thomas, salt of the earth, *pray for us.*
Saint Thomas, most illustrious light of the world, *pray for us.*
Saint Thomas, most firm pillar of the Church, *pray for us.*
Saint Thomas, wise as an angel of God hath wisdom, *pray for us.*
Saint Thomas, unconquerable refuter of heresies, *pray for us.*
Saint Thomas, most learned expounder of mysteries, *pray for us.*

Sancte Thoma, intérpres divínæ voluntátis, *ora pro nobis*.
Sancte Thoma, sanctíssimæ Eucharístiæ defénsor et cultor devotíssime, *ora pro nobis*.
Sancte Thoma, spíritu intelligéntiæ repléte, *ora pro nobis*.
Sancte Thoma, ad justítiam erúdiens multos, *ora pro nobis*.
Sancte Thoma, tamquam imbres mittens elóquia sapiéntiæ tuæ, *ora pro nobis*.
Sancte Thoma, de Deo sic loquens, quasi vidísses, *ora pro nobis*.
Sancte Thoma, de Angelis sic dísputans, quasi spíritus esses, *ora pro nobis*.
Sancte Thoma, ingénerans horrórem peccáti, dum osténdis, *ora pro nobis*.
Sancte Thoma, amábiles fáciens virtútes, dum descríbis, *ora pro nobis*.
Sancte Thoma, Incarnátum Verbum sic éxplicans, quasi vox Verbi, *ora pro nobis*.
Sancte Thoma, de veritáte doctrínæ tuæ ore Crucifíxi cértior facte, *ora pro nobis*.
Sancte Thoma, bonum Christi odórem in omni loco diffúndens, *ora pro nobis*.
Sancte Thoma, in lecto mortis ad erudiéndam Ecclésiam laboráre non recúsans, *ora pro nobis*.[1]
Sancte Thoma, ad mortem sancte te dispónens, *ora pro nobis*.

---

[1] This refers to Saint Thomas agreeing, in spite of the weakness caused by his approaching death, to expound the Canticle of Canticles at the request of the monks of Fossa Nova.

Saint Thomas, interpreter of the divine will, *pray for us.*
Saint Thomas, most devout defender and worshipper of the Most Holy Eucharist, *pray for us.*
Saint Thomas, filled with the spirit of understanding, *pray for us.*
Saint Thomas, who dost instruct many to justice, *pray for us.*
Saint Thomas, who didst pour forth the words of thy wisdom as showers, *pray for us.*
Saint Thomas, who didst speak of God as if thou hadst seen him, *pray for us.*
Saint Thomas, who didst treat of the angels as if thou wert a spirit, *pray for us.*
Saint Thomas, who dost beget a horror of sin when thou dost describe it, *pray for us.*
Saint Thomas, who dost render the virtues loveable when thou dost describe them, *pray for us.*
Saint Thomas, who didst treat of the Incarnate Word as if thou wert the voice of the Word, *pray for us.*
Saint Thomas, made more certain of the truth of thy teaching by the mouth of the Crucified, *pray for us.*
Saint Thomas, pouring forth the good odor of Christ in every place, *pray for us.*
Saint Thomas, who on thy deathbed didst not refuse to labor to instruct the Church, *pray for us.*[1]
Saint Thomas, who didst piously prepare thyself for death, *pray for us.*

Sancte Thoma, ante et post óbitum miráculis decoráte, *ora pro nobis.*

Sancte Thoma, fulgens quasi stella in perpétuas æternitátes, *ora pro nobis.*

Sancte Thoma, ut non diligámus mundum, neque ea quæ in mundo sunt, *ora pro nobis.*

Sancte Thoma, ut non quærámus homínibus placére, sed Deo, *ora pro nobis.*

Sancte Thoma, ut per bona ópera certam nostram vocatiónem et electiónem faciámus, *ora pro nobis.*

Sancte Thoma, ut nosípsos castos custodiámus, *ora pro nobis.*

Sancte Thoma, ut in castitátis certámine constitúti, non simus fidéntes in nobis, sed in Deo, *ora pro nobis.*

Sancte Thoma, ut scuto fídei ómnia tela nequíssimi ígnea exstinguámus, *ora pro nobis.*

Sancte Thoma, ut vigilémus, omni témpore orántes, *ora pro nobis.*

Sancte Thoma, ut carnem nostram crucifigámus cum vítiis et concupiscéntiis, *ora pro nobis.*

Sancte Thoma, ut simus húmiles in óculis nostris, agnoscéntes nos esse servos inútiles, *ora pro nobis.*

Sancte Thoma, ut alta non sapiámus, nec simus prudéntes apud nosmetípsos, *ora pro nobis.*

Sancte Thoma, ut doctrínis váriis et peregrínis non sinámus nos abdúci, *ora pro nobis.*

Sancte Thoma, ut ostendámus ex bona conversatióne operatiónem nostram in mansuetúdine sapiéntiæ, *ora pro nobis.*

Saint Thomas, adorned with miracles before and after death, *pray for us.*
Saint Thomas, shining as a star for all eternity, *pray for us.*
Saint Thomas, that we may not love the world nor those things that are in the world, *pray for us.*
Saint Thomas, that we may seek to please not men but God, *pray for us.*
Saint Thomas, that by good works we may make sure our calling and election, *pray for us.*
Saint Thomas, that we may preserve ourselves chaste, *pray for us.*
Saint Thomas, that in the midst of the battle for chastity, we may trust not in ourselves but in God, *pray for us.*
Saint Thomas, that with the shield of faith we may extinguish all the fiery darts of the most wicked one, *pray for us.*
Saint Thomas, that we may watch, praying at all times, *pray for us.*
Saint Thomas, that we may crucify our flesh, with the vices and concupiscences, *pray for us.*
Saint Thomas, that we may be humble in our own eyes, acknowledging ourselves to be unprofitable servants, *pray for us.*
Saint Thomas, that we may not mind high things nor be wise in our own conceits, *pray for us.*
Saint Thomas, that we may not allow ourselves to be led away with various and strange doctrines, *pray for us.*
Saint Thomas, that we may shew, by a good conversation, our work in the meekness of wisdom, *pray for us.*

Sancte Thoma, ut nobis peténtibus detur desúrsum sapiéntia modésta, suadíbilis, plena misericórdia, et frúctibus bonis, *ora pro nobis.*
Sancte Thoma, ut efficiámur operárii inconfusíbiles, recte tractántes verbum veritátis, *ora pro nobis.*
Sancte Thoma, ut in nobis non sciéntia inflans, sed cáritas ædíficans júgiter augeátur, *ora pro nobis.*
Sancte Thoma, ut sciámus Jesum Christum, et hunc crucifíxum, *ora pro nobis.*
Sancte Thoma, ut, tuum exémplum sequéntes, sanctíssimi Sacraménti cultum ac veneratiónem verbo et ópere promoveámus, *ora pro nobis.*
Sancte Thoma, ut sacro Viático in hora mortis refécti, fídei et devotiónis tuæ simus partícipes, *ora pro nobis.*
Sancte Thoma, ut Jesum, quem velátum aspícimus in via, reveláta fácie tecum cernámus in pátria, *ora pro nobis.*

Agnus Dei, qui tollis peccáta mundi, *parce nobis Dómine.*
Agnus Dei, qui tollis peccáta mundi, *exáudi nos Dómine.*
Agnus Dei, qui tollis peccáta mundi, *miserére nobis.*
Christe audi nos.
Christe exáudi nos.

Saint Thomas, that to we who ask may be given from above the wisdom that is modest, easy to be persuaded, full of mercy and good fruits, *pray for us.*

Saint Thomas, that we may be made workmen that need not to be ashamed, rightly handling the word of truth, *pray for us.*

Saint Thomas, that not the knowledge that puffeth up but charity that edifieth may always be increased in us, *pray for us.*

Saint Thomas, that we may know Jesus Christ, and him crucified, *pray for us.*

Saint Thomas, that following thy example, we may advance the worship and veneration of the Most Blessed Sacrament by word and work, *pray for us.*

Saint Thomas, that restored by the Sacred Viaticum at the hour of our death, we may be partakers of thy faith and devotion, *pray for us.*

Saint Thomas, that we may see Jesus, whom we behold veiled in the way, with open face in the homeland, *pray for us.*

Lamb of God, who takest away the sins of the world, *spare us, O Lord.*

Lamb of God, who takest away the sins of the world, *graciously hear us, O Lord.*

Lamb of God, who takest away the sins of the world, *have mercy on us.*

Christ, hear us.

Christ, graciously hear us.

Antiphona. O Doctor óptime, Ecclésiæ sanctæ lumen, beáte Thoma, divínæ legis amátor, deprecáre pro nobis Fílium Dei.

℣. Justum dedúxit Dóminus per vias rectas.
℞. Et osténdit illi regnum Dei.

Orémus.

Deus, qui Ecclésiam tuam beáti Thomæ, Confessóris tui, mira eruditióne claríficas, et sancta operatióne fecúndas: da nobis, quǽsumus, et quæ dócuit intelléctu conspícere, et quæ egit imitatióne complére. Per Dóminum nostrum Jesum Christum Fílium tuum, qui tecum vivit et regnat in unitáte Spíritus Sancti Deus: per ómnia sǽcula sæculórum. ℞. Amen.

Dómine Jesu Christe, Fili Dei vivi, puritátis amátor et custos, obsecrámus imménsam cleméntiam tuam: ut sicut ministério Angelórum sanctum Thomam Aquinátem cíngulo castitátis cíngere, atque a labe córporis et ánimæ præservári voluísti, ita nos, ejus méritis et intercessióne, ab omni immundítia mentis et córporis purificári, atque in éxitu nostro per manus sanctórum Angelórum tibi digne præsentári concédas: Qui cum Patre et Spíritu Sancto vivis et regnas Deus, per ómnia sǽcula sæculórum. ℞. Amen.

Antiphon. O most eminent Doctor, light of holy Church, blessed Thomas, lover of the divine law, pray for us to the Son of God.

℣. The Lord conducted the just through the right ways.
℟. And shewed him the kingdom of God.

Let us pray.

O God, who makest thy Church glorious through[2] the wonderful learning of blessed Thomas, thy Confessor, and renderest her fruitful by his holy actions; grant us, we beseech thee, clearly to understand the things which he taught, and faithfully to imitate what he performed. Through our Lord Jesus Christ thy Son, who liveth and reigneth with thee, in the unity of the Holy Ghost God, for ever and ever. ℟. Amen.

Lord Jesus Christ, Son of the living God, lover and guardian of purity, we beseech thy immense clemency, that as thou didst will by the ministry of angels to bind Saint Thomas Aquinas with the cincture of chastity and that he be preserved from stain of body and soul: so by his merits and intercession, grant that we may be purified from all uncleanness of mind and body and, at our death, worthily presented to thee by the hands of the holy angels. Thou who livest and reignest with the Father and the Holy Ghost God, for ever and ever. ℟. Amen.

---

[2] This could also be rendered: who dost enlighten thy Church with...

Postquam Coloniæ sub Alberto Magno in sacris studijs non
mediocriter profecisset, Lutetiam venit anno Domini MCCXLVI.
vbi Doctoris nomine et munere, anno ætatis tricesimo insig=
nitus est: in quo ita toto vitæ suæ tempore versatus est,
vt toto terrarum orbi egregia eruditionis monumenta reliquerit.

THE SIX SUNDAYS IN HONOR OF SAINT THOMAS AQUINAS

This devotion consists in offering prayers, meditations, or other devotions in honor of Saint Thomas Aquinas on six consecutive Sundays. It was originally approved by Pope Leo XIII for the Sundays preceding or following his feast, March 7. Though this is the most fitting time to keep this devotion, it can be kept at other times during the year, such as before or after January 28, the feast of the translation of his relics, or November 13, the feast of his patronage over Catholic schools. No specific prayers were prescribed, but the following were composed by Father Henry Joseph Pflugbeil to accompany the meditations in his book, the "St. Thomas Manual."

.....

FIRST SUNDAY
SAINT THOMAS'S EARLY YEARNINGS AFTER GOD

O angelic teacher, Saint Thomas of Aquin, thou didst early begin to seek that which alone is worth the efforts of an immortal spirit! That thou wast permitted to gaze so far into the abyss of God's infinite perfections, is no marvel to me; since even in thy childhood thou didst, like a young eagle fix thine eyes upon the radiance of his divine splendor. O how happy should I be if like thee my early affections had all been given to God, and again like thee I had been true to my first love! And yet even now I may count myself happy if, under thy guidance, I run on unshackled by the things of earth and, at last, reach the Supreme Good. Nothing, nothing shall now impede my progress. If my state in life forbids the absolute resignation of exterior things, it cannot prevent the entire detachment of my heart from them. Exultingly as the lark on a summer morn, shall my heart soar up to God, to breathe the pure air whence thou didst draw such abundance of grace, and near thee to learn how pitiful is all that is not God.

Obtain for me the grace, O my angelic guide, to love God above all things, not merely in word, but in heart and in deed. I am sincerely resolved to live for him, to die for him. But I know my weakness to be such that without heavenly assistance my resolve can produce no lasting effects. Ah then, be thou my special protector and guide on the way to God. Obtain that like thee, my saintly model, I may sigh for no other reward in the toils of this life than God alone for all eternity! Amen.

.....
SECOND SUNDAY
SAINT THOMAS'S LOVE OF CHASTITY

O holy, innocent master, thou leader of the host pure of soul, I now begin to understand what gained for thee the title, "Angel of the Schools." The eye of an angel must indeed be able to contemplate that which constitutes an angel's blessedness. Well didst thou understand that saying of the Holy Ghost: "Wisdom will not enter into a malicious soul, nor dwell in a body subject to sins." — Thou hast told me that the heart that gives itself up to sensuality must be weak, bad, and subject to low instincts. I believe thee, and I will follow thy counsels. Never will I have aught to do with what might endanger the lovely, the precious purity of my soul. When the tempter suddenly appears, may I like thee in the hour of thy fiery and memorable victory, seize the flaming brand of holy love with which to put my enemy to flight! I solemnly promise thee, O my holy leader, to flee from every shadow of danger, to be watchful in the choice of my books, my friends, my conversations, my recreations, yes, even in my food and drink as far as in me lies.

But do thou, O heavenly protector, obtain for me the divine assistance in those encounters from which so few come forth victorious. I will conquer, I must conquer! Protect me from whatever could wound purity in the least degree and keep me in the love of this beautiful virtue till the end, that I may belong to those who in heaven thank thee for thy guard over them and contribute to thy glory, O thou triumphant leader and renowned hero of virginity! Amen.

.....
THIRD SUNDAY
THE SOLID HUMILITY OF SAINT THOMAS

O great Saint Thomas, radiant, magnificent star of Holy Church, who wast at the same time so humble and modest, thou wast entirely free from the sting of that horrible and grievous vice which thou didst so clearly portray as the most frightful wandering, as the greatest estrangement from God, and the most deplorable of all sins! O how confused am I at the sight of thy greatness which knew so well how to humble itself! Yes, thou art the teacher of truth, for thou didst practice the truth thou didst proclaim in terms so touchingly beautiful! Humility is truth. Humility is the acknowledgment that we deserve degradation only, and that honor belongs to God alone.

O help me, Saint Thomas, not to comprehend something of this truth, for it is so clear that only the insanity of pride could fail to see it; but help me to practice it, since I cannot do that without great grace. Hardly does a humiliation menace me, when I begin to shrink from it; my pride rises up; reasons are multiplied against it; and I leave no means untried, how suspicious soever they may be, in order to avert the dreaded calamity.

Ah, have pity on me! Fail not to assist me as often as my stupid pride gets the mastery and leads me to behave in a manner so unworthy of a scholar of him who was God, but who at the same time said: "Learn of me, because I am meek, and humble of heart." — Full of confidence in thine assistance, O humble and yet mighty protector, I will daily practice those virtues that, for the very reason of thy greatness, shine so conspicuously in thee, O thou man of giant intellect, thou infallible teacher of the Church, thou renowned oracle of our day! O great and humble Saint Thomas, make me as humble as thyself!

FOURTH SUNDAY
SAINT THOMAS'S INDEFATIGABLE ARDOR IN THE SEARCH AFTER SACRED WISDOM

"GOD OF MY FATHERS, AND LORD OF MERCY, who hast made all things with thy word, and by thy wisdom hast appointed man, that he should have dominion over the creature that was made by thee: give me wisdom, that sitteth by thy throne, and cast me not off from among thy children: for I am thy servant, and the son of thy handmaid, a weak man, and of short time, and falling short of the understanding of judgment and laws. Send her out of thy holy heaven, and from the throne of thy majesty, that she may be with me, and may labour with me, that I may know what is acceptable with thee: for by wisdom they were healed, whosoever have pleased thee, O Lord, from the beginning." (Wisdom IX, 1, 2, 4, 5, 10, 19).

Thou didst, O Lord, fill thy servant, Saint Thomas, with incomparable, heavenly wisdom, so that in very truth, can the whole Church satiate her hunger with the fruits of his works! Give me a little spark of his illumination signified by the sun upon his breast. Give me a ray of his celestial light that by it my path through life may be lit up and that, if it be thy holy will, I may enkindle it in others.

Pray for me, O great and wonderful master, that I may imitate thee in this wherein all may follow thine example, that I may keep my eyes always turned heavenward. As the eagle seizes its young and bears it on high, in order to sharpen its gaze by fixing it upon the sun; so do thou raise me up, that mine eyes may now become accustomed to look upon the Sun of eternal brightness and thence to draw eternal happiness. Obtain for me, Saint Thomas, what the Church bids me ask on thy feast: namely, to understand what thou didst teach, and in my life to follow what thou didst practice. Through Christ, our Lord. Amen.

.....
FIFTH SUNDAY
SAINT THOMAS &
THE MOST BLESSED SACRAMENT

O glorious bard of the Most Blessed Mystery of our altars, Saint Thomas![1] How shall I praise thee and love thee as thou deservest for having placed before us, in all its majesty and beauty, the great Mystery of the love of Jesus Christ, for having shown us in thine own life how to venerate that miracle of God's power! Thou thyself dost serve us as a model in this. From the glowing treasures of thine own heart, thou dost place upon our lips the words most fitting and most beautiful, with which we are to praise, to magnify, to adore, and to love this highest and holiest of all the Sacraments. Thy thoughts, thy words, thy labors, thy whole life, form one continuous "Pange lingua," one unbroken "Adóro te." Though hast enabled us in those heavenly

---

[1] Saint Thomas composed the liturgical texts for Corpus Christi.

sounds to do homage to our God upon earth, to hail him in songs of joy. They truly express the praises of the angelic throng, since they come to us from thy lips, O thou angel upon earth!

O help me, angelic master, that the Bread of Angels, of which thou singest:

> Lo! upon the altar lies,
> Hidden deep from human eyes,
> Bread of angels from the skies,
> Made the food of mortal man;
> Children's meat to dogs denied

may be in very deed to me the "Children's Bread!" Stand by me, teach me, and obtain for me the divine assistance, that I may not draw upon myself a refusal when I sing before the Most Blessed Sacrament thy words: "Sic nos tu vísita, sicut te cólimus," "Do thou visit us, even as we honor thee."—With heart and lips will I repeat the words, seeking day by day to understand them better, which Holy Church from thee learned and has already rehearsed innumerable times:

O God, who hast left us in this wonderful Sacrament a perpetual memorial of thy Passion: grant us, we beseech thee, so to reverence the sacred mysteries of thy Body and Blood, that we may continually find in our soul the fruit of thy Redemption: Thou who livest and reignest, world without end. Amen.

SIXTH SUNDAY
SAINT THOMAS'S LOVE FOR THE BLESSED VIRGIN MARY

O Mary, glorious Mother of Jesus Christ, most pure Virgin, powerful Queen of heaven! Behold I come to thee sorrowful for my past infidelity. As to Saint Thomas, so also to me hast thou given rich graces and blessings, yes, long before I could begin to salute thee; and thou didst not cease to love me long after I had grown tepid and negligent in thy service. O do not now abandon me, since my saintly master has opened my eyes to see again how happy thy children are under thy protecting mantle and near thy pure heart! Now will I remain unshaken in my fidelity to thee, untiring in my efforts to bring others to thee; now will I constantly aim at procuring thee and thy children honor. Forsake me not, O Mother of Mercy! Thou art the Mother and special patroness of the Order whose brightest ornament Saint Thomas, under thy maternal assistance, became. Behold, I too will become a spiritual child of this holy family, whose chief duty it is to preach Jesus Crucified and, by their glowing words, to enkindle in the hearts of the faithful ardent love for thee, his Mother. As far as I can, I will engrave in all hearts, but first of all in my own, thy name in ineffaceable characters.

And do thou, O holy, angelic master, thou the scholar, the lover, the preacher, the sacred doctor of Mary, do thou teach me to love Mary with that pure, intelligent, faithful, and persevering love with which thou, from thine early childhood until thy last hour, didst love her and of which thou didst give her daily and tender proofs! Ah, then, when I go into "the house of my eternity," I shall, in ecstasy of soul and jubilation of heart, pronounce that "Ave Maria," that sweet salutation, which produced so great an impression upon thee before thine infant tongue could lisp its accents![2]

---

[2] This refers to an incident when Saint Thomas was still an infant. When trying to bathe him, his nurse could not get him to let go of a slip of paper in his hand. When his mother managed to take it from him, it was found to have the words "Ave Maria" written upon it. The child consumed the paper once it was returned to him. The Breviary interprets this as a foreshadowing of his great devotion to Our Lady.

Intrat cubiculum eius D. Bonauentura, qui ei semper in studijs et pietate collega exstitit, videt ille Thomam magna attentione abreptum, ei scribendo occupatum, ac Spiritum sanctum in columbæ specie et ad aures adstantem, qui ei quæ scribenda erant dictaret: quo viso, D. Bonauentura, nequod impedimentum scribendi daret, statim se cubiculo proripit.

SOURCES

The New Raccolta, or, Collection of Prayers and Good Works to Which the Sovereign Pontiffs Have Attached Holy Indulgences. Peter F. Cunningham, 1903. https://archive.org/details/TheNewRaccolta/page/444/mode/2up.

Christopher, Joseph P., Charles E. Spence, and John F. Rowan. *The Raccolta; or, A Manual of Indulgences, Prayers and Devotions Enriched with Indulgences.* Benziger Brothers, 1957.

Bernard Gui. "Vita S. Thomæ Aquinatis." In *Fontes vitæ S. Thomæ Aquinatis, notis historicis et criticis illustrati*, edited by Dominic Prümmer, 161–263. Privately published in Toulouse, 1912. https://archive.org/details/fontesvitaesthom00pr/page/160/mode/2up.

Fanfani, Louis. *De Confraternitatibus aliisque associationibus Ordini FF. Prædicatorum propriis.* Rome: Apud Domum Generalem, 1934.

Gowing, George Joseph. *Horæ sacræ: Preces et exercitia devotionis per diem, aliquotiesve faciendæ et speculum meditantis seu sacerdos sanctificatus, ad vitam sacerdotalem pie instituendam tractatus.* London, 1878. https://books.google.co.uk/books?id=4SD724wWjyAC&printsec=frontcover.

Pflugbeil, Henry Joseph. *St. Thomas Manual: or, Devotion of the Six Sundays in Honor of the Angel of the Schools, St. Thomas of Aquin.* New York, 1887. Facsimile reprint by Sagwan Press, 2018.

Saint John, Ambrose, trans. *The Little Office of St. Thomas Aquinas.* Sixth edition. Burns and Oates, 1909. Bodleian Library shelf mark 13829 f.15.

Suarez, Emmanuel. *Breviarium juxta ritum S. Ordinis Prædicatorum ad normam bullæ "Divino afflatu" et motu proprio "Abhinc duos annos" fel. rec. Pii PP. X reformatum, apostolica auctoritate appropatum.* 2 volumes. Rome: Ad S. Sabinam, 1947.

William of Tocco. "Vita S. Thomæ Aquinatis." In *Fontes vitæ S. Thomæ Aquinatis, notis historicis et criticis illustrati*, edited by Dominic Prümmer, 57–160. Privately published in Toulouse, 1912. https://archive.org/details/fontesvitaesthomo0opr/page/56/mode/2up.

The frontispiece is a print by Michel Natalis after a design by Abraham van Diepenbeeck, published by Martinus van den Enden, Antwerp, 1620–1668, housed at the Rijksmuseum and accessible at https://id.rijksmuseum.nl/200237230. The engravings on pp. iv, viii, x, xv, xvi, 84, and 94 are taken from the *Vita D. Thomae Aquinatis*, a collection of thirty engravings by Cornelis Boel after a design by Otto van Veen, published in Antwerp in 1610. The complete set may be found at https://commons.wikimedia.org/wiki/Category:Vita._D.Thomae_Aquinatis_/_Othonis_Vaeni_ingenio_et_manu_delineata. All images are in the public domain.

www.ingramcontent.com/pod-product-compliance
Lightning Source LLC
Chambersburg PA
CBHW072117050526
44107CB00120BA/1375/J